Children's Literature for All God's Children

Virginia Coffin Thomas
Betty Davis Miller

John Knox Press
ATLANTA

Unless otherwise indicated, Scripture quotations are from the Revised Standard Version of the Holy Bible, copyright, 1946, 1952, and © 1971, 1973 by the Division of Christian Education, National Council of the Churches of Christ in the U.S.A. and used by permission.

Acknowledgment is made for permission to quote from the following sources:

To Atheneum Publishers, Inc. for material from Joseph Krumgold, excerpt from *Henry Three*. Copyright © 1967 Joseph Krumgold. Reprinted with the permission of Atheneum Publishers, Inc.

To Cambridge University Press for material from AN EXPERIMENT IN CRITICISM by C. S. Lewis. Copyright © 1961. Reprinted by permission of Cambridge University Press.

To Delacorte Press for material from CHOOSING BOOKS FOR CHILDREN by Betsy Hearne. Copyright © 1981. Reprinted by permission of Delacorte Press.

To E. P. Dutton, Inc. for material from GATES OF EXCELLENCE by Katherine Paterson. Copyright © 1981. Reprinted by permission of E. P. Dutton, Inc.

To Farrar, Straus & Giroux, Inc. for material from TUCK EVERLASTING by Natalie Babbitt. Copyright © 1975. Reprinted by permission of Farrar, Straus and Giroux.

To Harcourt Brace Jovanovich, Inc. for excerpts from ITALIAN FOLKTALES Italo Calvino, copyright © 1956 by Giulio Einaudi editore, s.p.a.; English translation copyright © 1980 by Harcourt Brace Jovanovich, Inc. Reprinted by permission of Harcourt Brace Jovanovich, Inc. For excerpts from HALF MAGIC by Edward Eager, copyright 1954 by Harcourt Brace Jovanovich, Inc.; renewed 1982 by Jane Eager. Reprinted by permission of the publisher. For excerpts from A STRANGER AT GREEN KNOWE by L. M. Boston.

Copyright © 1962. Reprinted by permission of Harcourt Brace Jovanovich, Inc.

To Harper & Row, Publishers, Inc. for specified excerpt from page 183 of CHARLOTTE'S WEB by E. B. White and illustrated by Garth Williams. Copyright 1952 by E. B. White; text copyright renewed © 1980 by E. B. White. Specified excerpt from pages 1 and 2 of THE BEST CHRISTMAS PAGEANT EVER by Barbara Robinson. Copyright © 1972 by Barbara Robinson. Specified excerpt (pages 1, 235) from . . .AND NOW MIGUEL by Joseph Krumgold (Thomas Y. Crowell). Copyright © 1953 by Joseph Krumgold. Specified excerpt from page 4 of DRAGONWINGS by Laurence Yep. Copyright © 1975 by Laurence Yep. Specified excerpt from pages 225 and 276 of HARRIET THE SPY by Louise Fitzhugh. Copyright © 1964 by Louise Fitzhugh. All selections reprinted by permission of Harper & Row, Publishers, Inc.

To Random House, Inc. for material from THE PHANTOM TOLLBOOTH by Norton Juster. Copyright © 1964. Reprinted by permission of Random House, Inc.

To William Morrow & Company, Inc. for excerpts, as scattered quotes, from pp. 34, 111–112, 113–114 in RAMONA THE BRAVE by Beverly Cleary. Copyright © 1975 by Beverly Cleary. For excerpt from page 63 in RAMONA AND HER FATHER by Beverly Cleary. Copyright © 1975, 1977, by Beverly Cleary. By permission of William Morrow & Company.

Library of Congress Cataloging-in-Publication Data

Thomas, Virginia, 1926—
    Children's literature for all God's children.

    Includes bibliographies and index.
    1. Christian literature for children. 2. Christian literature for children—Bibliography. I. Miller, Betty Davis. II. Title.
BR117.5.T47   1986   268'.6   85-17169
ISBN 0-8042-1690-8

Acknowledgments

No work is done in a vacuum. We could begin by thanking our ancestors, both physical and literary, for all that has gone before. We write this acknowledgment in that spirit, realizing the contributions made by parents, teachers, ministers, friends, relatives, authors, and children who have shared books with us. In a more specific vein we thank our husbands, who served as critics and proofreaders, and our own children, who taught us more than we ever taught them. We thank P. C. Ennis, Jr., Joseph Harvard, Robert E. Knox, Jr., Mary Jean McFadyen, and George Telford for reading our manuscript in various stages and making valuable comments; Lamar Williamson, Jr. for answering questions and guiding us to some excellent resources on biblical criticism; and Thomas G. Long, Jr. for an introduction to inductive preaching; and David Garth and Davis Thomas for sermon examples. Before and during our writing we have turned continuously to the shelves and children's librarians of the following library systems: Leon County, Florida; Volusia County, Florida; Tampa-Hillsborough, Florida; and Vancouver, Washington.

To our husbands, our children, and our grandchildren.
For teachers and ministers in the church and all children
whose lives and hearts will be touched by these stories.

Contents

Dear Educator, Leader, Pastor, Parent, Grandparent, Church Librarian, Pilgrim, Seeker, Communicator, Witness:

You hold in your hand a book about bridges—bridges between the Bible and contemporary life, between faith and action, between the church and the world, and between children and adults. These bridges will take us into learning, into worship, and into the marvelous world of childhood. We are speaking of the books and stories usually designated "the literature of childhood."

Most likely you are an adult, responsible for such matters as sermons, educational plans, committee meetings, family budgets, and the ethics of economics and politics. You may be tempted to stop reading now, feeling that children's books are too frail a span to support the steps of one weighted with such concerns.

We write because we have found the stories children love to be a sure way across mountains of dullness, rivers of irrelevance, swamps of fuzzy abstractions, and chasms dividing age groups. We did not make this discovery quickly or easily. Our convictions have been forming for over fifty years (twenty-five apiece).

We began our conversations about books as we served together in the church nursery. Between diapers, snacks, tears, and toys we sandwiched ideas about children, husbands, homes, faith, and good reading. We did not always agree, but one thing we shared in that situation has stood the test of time: the ability to continue a conversation through many interruptions.

Our children grew; we served in other ways in the church; residences changed; vocational aspirations took new forms. A constant was our conversation about books, increasingly about children's books. We had always read to our children (and still read to our grandchildren). Now we began to share books with other children in two different settings, one The State Library of Florida, the other the church. What became increasingly apparent through these years was how frequently good literature was related to good Christian education. At this point our conversation became purposeful enough to become a book.

Think of this book as a continuation of our conversation, with several participants added. Some of your voices will be heard, for we are responding to questions asked us by ministers, educators, and parents as well as to questions we have asked each other. Books and authors will add their words. We will introduce these as they join the conversation, and you can find more about them in the bibliographies.

Our answers and ideas may be incomplete or even (humility dictates this inclusion) incorrect, but they have all grown out of specific needs and situations. We know from experience the worth of children's literature, and we are convinced that good books for children are a rich and untapped resource for proclaiming and interpreting the Christian faith to all ages. We are sure that these stories belong in the library of anyone concerned with Christian communications. Both old and young can be enriched by their content and can learn from their style. We hope that what we have to say will be a bridge for you into the faith-expanding experience of the literature of childhood.

Conversations do not lend themselves to strict outlines, but this one touches on four general areas: why children's literature is a good resource for Christians; some insights we gain about children and communication from these books; ways to learn about and share children's literature; and two bibliographies, one for all ages and one for adults. If you are discerning enough to be reading this book, then you are certainly wise enough to refer to the various sections as you need them.

Perhaps a few words of introduction will help to start the conversation.

Virginia has taught all ages of children in the church and has spoken and written widely on the subject of children and worship. Her husband, a retired Presbyterian minister, has been a sounding board and test case for many of her ideas about children's books in the church. You will hear her voice in the first chapter as she draws on her experiences in the church to begin the conversation about problems in communicating our faith.

Betty is the Youth Services Consultant for the State Library of Florida. She and her husband, a professor at Florida State University, live in Tallahassee. She has served as elder, teacher, and Witness Council chair in the First Presbyterian Church there. She has written for the American Library Association about programming to promote reading and is a member of the 1984 Newbery Award Committee. Betty continues the conversation from the viewpoint of one who sees rich possibilities in children's literature.

So now, if you are ready, we have something to say. . . .

PART I
A Communication Bridge

Virginia begins the conversation by expressing the need for help in communicating the Christian faith through words. Her experiences in the church lead her to ask how we can strengthen the intergenerational community and go beyond idea to experience. Children's literature, Betty answers, can be such a bridge, because it transmits understanding and experience from one generation to the next in forms and styles that both children and adults understand. Although children's literature is not avowedly Christian, it is a valid and valuable resource for the church. The Bible and literature speak in common literary forms, in the language of analogy, and in answer to the universal questions of life. The stories of literature can extend and interpret the Story of the Bible.

1

The Need for Bridges

How can we communicate the Christian faith through words? Virginia begins the conversation:

In Norton Juster's *The Phantom Tollbooth*, Milo and Tock the Watchdog arrive in Dictionopolis on Monday which, by order of King Azaz the Unabridged, is always Word Market Day. Milo is usually bored with words, but today he is dazzled by the bountiful array. There are long, short, and easy words, special occasion words in fancy boxes, bags of pronouns, pounds of names, packages of adjectives, fresh-picked conjunctions and verbs, even bins of letters for the do-it-yourself customer. Milo is overcome with excitement:

"Look, Tock," he cried, "Aren't they wonderful."
"They're fine, if you have something to say," replied Tock in a tired voice . . . (47).

We see that words without content are meaningless. But what is it we wish to say? How do we wish to say it, and most importantly, why do we wish to speak? No matter what scholars say, there is something unsatisfactory about the ending of Mark's Gospel: ". . . they said nothing to any one, for they were afraid" (Mark 16:8). I understand the fear, but the silence is unbelievable. Somehow the resurrection called for proclamation. "Go and tell" is not only a command; it is an irresistible reaction to hearing the good news. The church is a people with something to say. We have a common calling to use words—teaching, preaching, telling, witnessing, announcing, and speaking the truth in love.

All we have to do is speak up. And that is where I encounter the problem illustrated in the following excerpts from conversations.

"I've decided talking about God isn't possible," said the teacher after three weeks of Christian doctrine with the senior high students. "Words are inadequate. 'Infinite,' 'eternal,' and 'unchangeable' just sort of sit there on the page."

"We've talked about Jesus welcoming all sorts of persons for three weeks now," lamented the elementary class teacher. "Yet when a shy, unattractive new student comes to class, the children simply ostracize her. There was absolutely no connection between what we said and the way they acted."

"I hate to mention stewardship," said the chairperson of the committee. "Before you can say 'I don't want to talk about money but about motives,' defenses are up."

The Family Camp committee argued through two fruitless meetings about the study sessions during the church retreat. "Either children won't understand what we say or adults will be bored. We just don't speak a common language."

The ministers in a workshop echo these sentiments. "It's hard enough to speak a common word to a congregation of differing cultural, educational, economic, and political preferences. Throw in the children and it's almost impossible."

"I wish there were something I could say that would help our youth see the consequences of some of their choices. I mean really see them. Without sounding like I'm speaking in some ancient language that no longer applies." A father expressed this yearning on the way to a youth retreat.

A member of the service committee struggled to interpret a mission concern in an affluent church: "It's hard to talk about poverty and homelessness in this church. We've simply never experienced it."

"Words like fellowship, salvation, life—they simply don't have much meaning to people I talk with at school," said a college student who was trying hard to articulate what the Christian faith meant to him.

Something beyond "speaking up" seems to be involved. These kinds of conversations occurred so frequently that I began to feel that speakers (usually adults) and audiences (children, youth, and adults) were standing on two sides of a vast chasm. Sermons, lessons, words of encouragement or warning shouted from one side reached the other only as indistinct echoes while the words fell in the vast space below.

Why? All of these people had something to say. The ideas were significant and life-shaping. The character of God, the life of Jesus, the responsible use of God's gifts, the meaning of faith and salvation are worth hearing about. Was the problem with the words? Were they inadequate to carry meaning from one person to another? Were they poorly chosen? Having something to say and saying it in a way that is inviting and understandable do not always go together. How can we communicate the Christian faith?

I agree with Milo. Words are wonderful. I like their sounds, their histories, their particular colors and feelings. I like them spoken, written, and sung. I think that observing a two-year-old entering the world of language is more exciting than sending a person to the moon. I marvel at these gifts which allow us to ask questions, share knowledge, express a need, tell a joke or a story, take a vow, and say "thank you" and "I love you."

Occasionally we hear contempt for speech as opposed to action, but the truth is that words *are* action. While we may abuse and misuse them, we cannot do without them. "Most people can find no meaning, no order, cannot even recognize their existence until they have formed their perceptions into words or found them reflected in someone else's words. St. John was only too right: in the beginning was the Word" (Chambers 1973, 7).

In *Walking on Water* Madeleine L'Engle, Christian and author, states the importance of words in another way: "We cannot Name or be Named without language. . . . When language becomes exhausted, our freedom dwindles" (39). I heard, and continue to hear the good news in words from the Bible. We are stuck with words and I am delighted. They are a marvelous gift, a tool for communication.

The trouble is that we have to decide how the tool will be used. Jesus promised we would be given the words to say when we stand before hostile governments and councils (and at times church school classes bear close resemblance to these), but for routine occasions we must exert ourselves to make choices. What words will we choose?

Like many Americans, I have been flirting with a personal computer lately. The investigation has done little for my comprehension and a lot for my vocabulary. "Word Plus" is one of the phrases that now rolls glibly from my tongue. Whatever it represents in the world of computers, it describes what I am looking for when we have something to say about our faith. We must choose and use words in such a way that they do more than entertain, inform, stimulate interest, raise money, or prompt to good works. Our words serve a Word seeking to turn us around, create new life, and bring in a new order.

We need a Word Plus in another sense. We are a family, a community of several generations. Whatever words we use must be inclusive and community-affirming. We know how difficult this task is when we look at what should be our most integrated experience, corporate worship. I have visualized a service with headphones like a United Nations forum. The minister preaches and, instead of selecting Russian, Arabic, or Spanish, the listeners dial to child, adolescent, or adult (young, middle, or senior) dialect. Each word would be translated into the listener's particular cognitive and emotional language. Yet, a community of worshipers isolated by headphones does not quite ring true.

We need a Word Plus because we must get beyond our own limited experience and viewpoints. The Christian community is multi-ethnic, multi-cultural. Our shrinking world brings us into contact with people who seem strange, alien, and sometimes hostile. It brings us into physical proximity with those whose ways are different, and thus tests the spiritual unity we have so easily professed. We need a unifying, peace-making word. We need a word that bridges the distance between speaker and listener, and between listeners of various ages and origins.

Each of the speakers in the conversations I have reported was seeking for a Word Plus: an effective, fruitful word. They all had something to say and they wanted it to be heard, to be used as a channel for the living Word. They were asking, "How can we use words so that communication occurs? How do words become bridges?"

I wish I could say that in each conversation I dispensed wisdom and solved problems. Unfortunately, such was not the case. What I can report, however, is an interesting pattern that emerged from my immediate and delayed responses.

In the first instance I joined in the lament about the inadequacy of words to convey anything about God. Later that week I caught a very quick glimpse of "unchangeable" in two books I read with the children. One was *The Runaway Bunny* by Margaret Wise Brown; the other was *The Horse and His Boy* from the Narnia series by C. S. Lewis.

I was the teacher in the second instance. I met one of my pupils in the school library where I assisted. Returning *The Hundred Dresses* by Eleanor Estes, she exclaimed, "It was the *best* book. It felt awful when they treated Wanda that way." What research, art, discussion, and music had failed to do was in a measure accomplished by a children's story.

"Let me suggest a story," I said to the friend who wrestled with stewardship. "It may be an opening wedge into some closed minds if it's done as a readers theater.

It certainly slipped up on me as I read it." I placed O'Dell's *The Black Pearl* in her hand.

A minister sent me a sermon on faithfulness. The introduction was from *Horton Hatches the Egg* by Dr. Seuss. I wished I had that book for both the family camp committee and the ministers at the workshop. Almost sure to be known by even the youngest in the group, it contains a story for everyone.

A troubled young person returned Burch's *Queenie Peavy* to the library. "I really know this girl," she said. "I can just see myself when she gets mad at everyone." I thought about the father who wanted to help young people see consequences before they occurred.

And then it hit me. When faced with a problem in effective communication, I repeatedly turned to a children's book. Why? What was it that pulled me to Horton, Narnia, and the Runaway Bunny? What had my friends found through the words of Eleanor Estes and Robert Burch that had been lacking in lesson plans and good advice? Was it just these books, or were there characteristics in the literature of childhood that equipped them to convey our messages with special clarity and impact?

At this point I said to Betty:

Can the literature of childhood help us to communicate the Christian faith? I know that some books for youngsters have done this. Are there enough such books to justify my thinking that children's literature is a valuable resource to draw from when we have something to say?

2

The Strong Span

Can the literature of childhood help us communicate the Christian faith? Betty continues with a positive answer:

Obviously, my response to this question is a strong affirmative, even though the problem of sharing with our children and each other those things we have learned and are learning about being a Christian will not be answered entirely by children's literature.

Jean Karl, who is the children's book editor at Atheneum Publishers, makes the point in her book, *From Childhood to Childhood,* that even though our learning is imperfect, nevertheless children's literature is one vehicle that transmits our understanding and insights "from one generation to the next: from childhood to childhood" (1970, xi).

Good children's books, she says (and I paraphrase), are written by adults who have not quite forgotten what it is that children need and want as they grow up. They are books written out of a sense of what is true and good and hopeful about the human experience, and they are written in a way that children can understand.

Not surprisingly, I endorse Ms. Karl's conclusions about the importance and benefit to children of a body of literature which they can call their own. Furthermore, this is a largely untapped source that adults should use when they wish to communicate with children.

We have talked frequently about how much we, as adults, learn from children's book. One extremely important area of learning is about children themselves. It is astonishing how much we forget about being a child once we have grown up. This literature keeps us aware of the intensely compressed experience of childhood. It points up developmental patterns from birth until coming of age.

And here our learning extends beyond childhood, for these stories which take us from childhood into maturity, a brief thirteen or fourteen years, become in a sense a metaphor of our own life-long journey, the journey of civilization toward maturity, and our journey toward oneness with God.

Not only that, but much of children's literature, if we would attend, awakens in us echoes of past feelings we should remember and nurture. The best literature is characterized by its tone of truth. Children's literature is no exception; it contains truth riddled with hope, wonder, beauty, a belief in the unexpected, the miraculous, even. All of this we lose at the peril of our souls. It seems to me that these are the elements that live and glow in the story of God's love for us. I think this is what Frederick Buechner is saying in his book, *The Gospel as Story: Tragedy, Comedy, and Fairy Tale* (1977).

Italo Calvino makes the same point in other words, as he concludes a two-year study of Italian folk tales. "Folktales are real," he says.

Taken all together, they offer, in their oft-repeated and constantly varying examinations of human vicissitudes, a general explanation of life preserved in the slow ripening of rustic consciences; these folk stories are the catalog of the potential destinies of men and women, especially for that stage in life when destiny is formed, i.e., youth, beginning with birth, which itself often foreshadows the future; then the departure from home, and, finally, through the trials of growing up, the attainment of maturity and the proof of one's humanity. This sketch, although summary, encompasses everything: the arbitrary divisions of humans, albeit in essence equal, into kings and poor people; the persecution of the innocent and their subsequent vindication, which are the terms inherent in every life; love unrecognized when first encountered and then no sooner experienced than lost; the common fate of subjection to spells, or having one's existence predetermined by complex and unknown forces. This complexity pervades one's entire existence and forces one to struggle to free oneself, to determine one's own fate; at the same time we can liberate ourselves only if we liberate other people, for this is a sine qua non of one's own liberation. There must be fidelity to a goal and purity of heart, values fundamental to salvation and triumph. There must also be beauty, a sign of grace that can be masked by the humble, ugly guise of a frog; and above all, there must be present the infinite possibilities of mutation, the unifying element in everything: men, beasts, plants, things (1980, xviii–xix).

For me, religion is the story of our spiritual quest. It is a story about journey: the stops along the way, the helps we need, the progress we make, the attempt to assimilate all the disparate parts into a pattern. It is an old story told over and over, and we need to illustrate the meaning with new stories about the human condition, about the way life is lived and can be lived and should be lived. It is true, hopeful, wonderful, and full of miracles. Good children's literature, too, is all of those things.

Therefore, we have hit on one good answer to the problem of communication. The literature of childhood can be an effective common language, because the genre contains stories we can all listen to and learn from together. It is full of incidents and characters that we can respond to with varying degrees of understanding as we study and worship as one body.

Stories and words have always been important to me. Ever since I first began to understand abstractions, I have loved the opening of the Gospel according to John: "In the beginning was the Word, and the Word was with God, and the Word was God." The resonances of that sentence, its rhythm, the meanings that leap and overlay and seep up from those words about the Word have never ceased to fascinate. They justify the action of the intellect. They provide a theological trilogy that has enriched my life: Idea first, then doing and telling. Lives can be changed and shaped when words pierce the heart of a listener. Such a change must have occurred when your young friend understood concretely what it meant to be excluded as she read Estes' *The Hundred Dresses*. I surmise that as a result, her appreciation of the inclusiveness of God's love grew.

One of the major differences in the cognitive patterns of adults and children is that of abstract versus concrete thinking. Children up to age eleven or twelve think only in concrete terms and images, but adults have the capacity to think both concretely and abstractly. Those who do both best seem to be our writers and poets. They make their abstractions from worldly, concrete details, and the very specificity with which they report these details lends credibility to their conclusions. Thus these writers help children bridge the gap between concrete and abstract in their cognitive development, and children learn how to synthesize and condense the essence of experience from a myriad of discrete happenings.

Since concreteness is a characteristic both of children's thinking and of excellent children's literature, it is a quality we should strive to recapture in our own speech and writing if we wish to be good communicators. Another essential quality of good literature for children is brevity. Children's literature, like poetry, tends to condense. It focuses on a single facet. Perhaps one of our mottoes should be "Keep it short."

We have mentioned already that children's literature is a bridge from childhood to childhood where we can learn what it is like to be a child again; we have said that it is full of hope and wonder and that its specificity insures that small details are able to convey the larger meaning. But how can we convince adults that all this is true?

I remember my own resistance to these truths when I was in library school. I would never have taken the course in children's literature had it not been required, and I certainly would never have believed that I would go back to studies after my library degree to specialize in children's services. Even though at the time I had children of my own, even though my favorite childhood birthday presents were books, even though my mother read to me long after I was able to read to myself, I was not drawn to explore the field of children's literature. It was not that I was insensitive to the lives beyond my own that lay hidden in books; I simply felt I had outgrown childish things.

Anyway, kiddy lit, as it was called, was required, and I was determined to graduate. It was then I discovered a world which, if it had existed twenty-five years before, I had forgotten. Books were so much more beautiful than I remembered, and instead of a few, there were hundreds of truly memorable books written with the delicacy and perception I had encountered when I read the masters of English literature in college. I discovered that wisdom and understanding and a droll sense of the ridiculous were deliciously imparted in books meant for children. I discovered I could enjoy them on my own, bringing to them my adult experience, and that I could enjoy them even more when I shared them with a child.

Now I find, because of my work, that I usually talk with children and adults who agree with me. They may not have shared my enforced conversion, but they have found between the covers of children's books much that is rare and wonderful. I am not suggesting (in spite of all this testimony) that adults choose children's literature as their major intellectual fare. However, I do think it is a friend well worth the cultivating. Children's literature is a friend that adults must know if they have contact with children, a friend they should know if they want to communicate with children effectively.

I know from my own experience the resistance of the

unconverted. Even if some adults are now persuaded that the bridge from childhood to childhood is broader and tougher than any skeptic would have supposed, some lingering reservations may check their steps to the juvenile section of the library. And even stronger hesitations may prevent these adults from accepting children's literature as a means to convey the story of the Bible. After all, these books are not avowedly Christian; their authors speak from diverse persuasions. Our potential converts may have many questions about the value of "secular" literature in the church's teaching ministry, about the connection between fairy tales and the Bible, about the relation of theology to fiction. I think we should say something about that.

3

A Reliable Route

Is children's literature a reliable resource? We join our voices to answer some questions about the relationship of literature and the Christian faith.

Perhaps we have launched this conversation from the wrong place. Because we saw several situations in the life of the church where using children's literature seemed appropriate and because we have identified qualities that are valuable, we are thinking of literature primarily as a resource.

We did not read initially with any thought of these books' teaching value. We read them for our own satisfaction and for that of our children. Even after our children could do most of their own reading, we continued to read them, because books like Bishop's *Twenty and Ten* or Speare's *The Bronze Bow* fit our time, our schedules, and a purse or diaper bag better than, say, *Les Miserables*.

Art, we think, like persons, resists friendships based on pragmatism. So let us discourage questions about use, resources, theological connections, and education—or at least postpone them. Let us read simply because literature has something to offer, a gift for each of us.

It may help here if we say what we mean by literature. Our own definition is "words chosen and arranged to give pleasure and to lead into a new understanding of life." Sometimes biographies, histories, and books of information can initiate a literary experience, indeed a very valuable experience, but their main purpose is to tell facts and present information. Literature, on the other hand, does something else: it creates, evokes, invites, and involves. This particular body of material includes fairy tales, folk tales, myths, legends, poetry, and fiction. Many of these gave pleasure and enlightenment long before they were written down. Some, such as myths, legends, and folk tales, were not originally intended for children, but children have adopted them because these stories meet their needs.

Most of us admit the human need for enlightenment; the need for pleasure may require some defense, since we are inclined to equate it with things that are immoral or fattening. One gift of literature may be an increased awareness of what real pleasure is. Screwtape, the senior devil and title character of the C. S. Lewis classic, counsels his nephew never to let his human "subject" enjoy a simple, genuine pleasure like hot chocolate, a long walk, or a good book, for such indulgence makes one particularly susceptible to the Enemy.

Whenever we are aesthetically satisfied by beauty, form, patterns, and images; delighted by surprise, incongruity, or vitality; opened to or disturbed by a new perspective on ourselves, our neighbors, and our world; or led to deeper compassion or a sense of unlimited possibilities, we know God is at work. All of this can happen to us as we read literature.

C. S. Lewis, who, as much as any Christian in this century, has used words to communicate the Christian faith, comes closest to expressing what we want to say in *An Experiment in Criticism*. He speaks of the words of literature as windows or doors and suggests that in reading we are seeking an "enlargement of our being" (1961, 137). He continues,

> But in reading great literature I become a thousand men and yet remain myself. . . . I see with a myriad eyes, but it is still I who see. Here, as in worship, in love, in moral action, and in knowing, I transcend myself; and am never more myself than when I do (141).

In a similar vein, we recommend reading simply because literature is one of God's good gifts.

Literature and the Bible Are Related in Form

Setting aside concern for theological content, we also recommend reading because God has spoken to us

9

in a literary form. Northrop Frye, the noted literary critic, has proposed in *The Educated Imagination* that the first several years of literature in schools should be a study of the Bible, for the Bible is the prevailing influence on western writing. Frye's excellent study of the Bible and literature, *The Great Code,* was prompted by a teaching career in which he found that most students have little knowledge or understanding of the Bible.

Our experience has been in the opposite direction. Remembering when we first seriously read and studied poetry, we recall how the Psalms and portions of Isaiah fairly jumped from the page with new vitality and meaning. Thus, we further advocate a study of literature as an avenue into God's Word.

An exciting emphasis in biblical studies today is the literary-critical approach. *How* the Bible speaks God's word becomes an important part of the message. In *Reformed Liturgy and Music,* Thomas G. Long of Princeton Seminary describes this emphasis as a radical shift in biblical interpretation, "a move from a concern with the history of a biblical text to a concern for poetics, the literary, and communicative impact of a text." The focus is on "the power of biblical texts to act in a literary fashion upon hearers and readers" (1983, 13). While sermons are not necessarily stories Long concludes, they do have story-like characteristics.

In the same journal David Buttrick, another homiletics professor, illustrates the importance of how a literary form works in parables. He speaks of a "traveling action in consciousness" rather than a single point or teaching. The parable is a literary form that "does" something. It places us first in a position of mastery, lets us enter the world on our terms, and then suddenly disrupts our world, so that we face a new world (1983, 17). Incidentally, in looking for an analogy to the work of parables, he turns to Lewis Carroll's *Alice in Wonderland.*

The Bible and literature tell their story in similar ways. Both invite us to experience rather than argument, involvement rather than intellectual reasoning. Jesus, of course, was a master at creating brief, memorable stories that slip past the defenses we ordinarily raise before painful truth. Perhaps his hearers listened because an unprincipled judge, a willful son, and unfair wages were not perceived as religious. These stories draw us; we forget to attend to our own reactions; and we arrive at a different place through an experience rather than through logic—sometimes in spite of logic.

A knowledge of literature, then, will help us in understanding how God communicates the Story, how the Bible speaks to us, and how we in a theologically consistent way may communicate with others. The form is part of the content of the biblical message; hence literary form merits our attention.

Literature and the Bible Are Related in Language

Literature and the Bible speak a common language, the language of analogy. Both must make the unseen visible by use of metaphor, simile, and imagery.

" 'Evangelicals distrust analogy and metaphor' " and instead rely on propositional statements to reveal God, according to Roger Lundin in a *Newsweek* article about inspirational romances for Christians (Woodward 1984, 69). Lundin, a Wheaton College English professor, attributes to this distrust the evangelicals' meager contribution to great literature.

A similar literal-mindedness gripped the member of a Presbyterian church school class who pounded the table for emphasis, proclaiming, "If the Bible says the little hills skipped like lambs, they skipped like lambs." Alas, when our primary text speaks of God as rock, fortress, consuming fire, and shepherd, we are too frequently literalists with impoverished imaginations. We *must* speak of God in analogies, and literature increases our fluency in this language.

The Bible and Literature Speak of Life

The Bible and literature speak of and to the same concerns: life, its meaning and problems. Dorothy Jean Furnish, whose *Exploring the Bible with Children* is an excellent guide for relating the Bible to life, makes this summary statement: "To teach the Bible is to talk about life. To talk about life (within the Christian community) is to teach the Bible" (1975, 81).

Some people have difficulty seeing fiction as a window on life. The first president of Wheaton College, for example, considered a novel to be "at best a well-told lie" (Woodward 1984, 69). Actually, a good story or novel makes life, real life, more accessible to us than does a newspaper or documentary. Those who struggle along with Katherine Paterson's Gilly Hopkins to give up false illusions, or with George MacDonald's Curdie to remain faithful when appearances deceive, or with Meg Murry (L'Engle, *A Wrinkle in Time*) to conquer overwhelming evil, will know something about life that neither statistics nor bare history can tell.

The author of fiction presents meaningful rather than chronological events and frames an experience in breadth and depth for our viewing. The jealousy between brothers, for example, is part of the human condition, from Cain to the Prodigal's brother. It is contemporary and feminine in Paterson's *Jacob Have I Loved,* 1981 Newbery winner. This encounter with an old story in a different setting and voice adds a new dimension to our understanding.

Literature enlarges the areas where we can see God at work and biblical truth applied. The questions that express humanity's search for meaning are the themes of Bible stories; these are the very questions which literature develops and explores. When we see these themes outside the pages of the Bible, our awareness of life's major questions increases. We are delivered from a prooftext mentality and are newly able to hear the whole story of the Bible.

All we have said so far applies to literature in general, and children's literature is no exception. The stories children love will help us see literary form and language, and these in turn can make us more open to the Bible. We are the losers when we confine literature to "secular" education.

The Bible and Literature Tell Stories

Children's literature has a special strength in helping us "hear" the Bible story. In these books the story form is visible, uncluttered, and clear.

It is important to remember that God does speak to us through stories. Not only is our own spiritual quest illumined by new stories, but when we approach this from the other side as God's quest for us we are still speaking of Story and stories. The Bible is a story of stories. We do not believe that its writing was accidental or that the formation of the canon was haphazard. The example of Jesus more than justifies our emphasis on story-method as part of the content of God's Word.

Our faith comes to us as a story, first oral history around a campfire, then as written tales. The Hebrew confessed his faith with a story—"A wandering Aramean was my father. . ." (Deut. 26:5)—and the early church wrote its creed as gospel narrative. The sermons of the Acts are primarily narrative, and this knowledge is influencing preaching today. The Christian church is made up of those who have heard God's story and have become part of the plot.

Stories Bond Communities

Stories are not only the medium of the message, but also the glue that binds with common experience to help create a community of sisters and brothers. The stories handed down between parents and children were part of the Hebrew identity and heritage, and are part of our Christian heritage today. Joshua set up twelve stones at the Jordan to make an occasion for a child's question that would elicit the story of the entry into Canaan. The Passover was a storytelling event. Christmas and Easter, when truly celebrated, are storytelling events also.

We recall a conversation with Ann Waldron, the author of *The Integration of Mary-Larkin Thornhill.* Ann had been invited to address a gathering in Philadelphia and had been seated beside a young librarian from China during the dinner preceding her speech. Language, age, culture, and ideology all seemed barriers. What would they talk about? "But we became fast friends instantly," Ann said. "We had both read *Little Women.*"

A weekend retreat for choir children and their parents provides another illustration of the way shared stories build community. On this retreat we were learning about Lent and Holy Week and preparing music for the season's worship. Someone, to the leader's dismay, brought along a television set for watching a two-part evening special. Against the leader's better judgment we gathered around to watch the first night. It was a good adaptation of C. S. Lewis' *The Lion, the Witch and the Wardrobe.*

At the close of the story on the second night, we were a different group. We had walked through the wardrobe door together, suffered Edmund's betrayal, sorrowed at Aslan's death, rejoiced at his return and the defeat of evil. The story was a profound commentary on the very theme we were to sing of during Holy Week, but the net result of sharing this story was greater than deepened insights. Our united seeing and listening added a new dimension to our work together. To this day, everyone on that retreat has a special feeling for each other.

Families who read aloud through snowbound evenings in pre–radio and television days experienced this bonding power of shared literature. Through stories, parents and children develop depths and strengths in their relationships and build a repertoire of characters, experiences, and phrases that will become reference points in future communication.

We see, then, in the Christian community, a place for good stories—Bible stories, certainly, and other written and oral stories which enrich Bible stories and give us a common fund of characters and situations. Children's literature does this for all ages. There is something here to be shared by the non-reader, the beginning reader, the young person, and the adult. The church today is increasingly aware of the importance of learning and worshiping as an intergenerational community. When we want to share and shape values we must do so across and between ages. From the writing of anthropologist Margaret Mead to that of church educator John Westerhoff, we read how essential are all three generations for real learning to occur.

A look at the books children love will help us see that the gap between generations is not as wide as we think. In needs and emotions children and adults are alike, erotic love being the exception. The universal questions adults ask are asked by children, though in a slightly different form. Madeleine L'Engle says that a good children's book is any book a child will read, and we see children make adult fare like fairy tales or Burnford's *The Incredible Journey* their own. Several years ago an adult friend called to recommend a priceless Christmas book, which turned out to be Barbara Robinson's *The Best Christmas Pageant Ever,* a staple in the juvenile fiction section for several years. C. S. Lewis summarizes the idea thus: "Juvenile taste is simply human taste" (1966, 41).

So because we are a people of a unique Book, a book that touches every aspect of life and speaks in a literary form, we want children's literature to have the widest audience in the church. We believe that in your reading you will find that the Book and books are related, and that the literature we read can be a doorway into the Bible as well as an extension of its truth.

The Bible and Literature Are Distinct

Now, though we see a strong relationship between the Bible and literature, we are certainly not equating the two. The Bible is clearly something other than and more than literature to us. For a number of reasons we do not even like the term "Christian literature." It is too hard to define.

Nor are we giving an official stamp of theological orthodoxy to the content of good children's literature. No good book we know—*Pilgrim's Progress* may be the exception—began as a treatise on Christian theology. When you have a point to make, you need a sermon, a tract, or a textbook. The Narnia Chronicles, it is true, touch on many basics of the Christian faith, but C. S. Lewis, describing in *Of Other Worlds* how the series began, says the first step was a series of images: "a faun carrying an umbrella, a queen on a sledge, a magnificent lion" (1966, 36). The stories of George MacDonald were a crucial point in the conversion of C. S. Lewis and the faith of G. K. Chesterton, and MacDonald says that he only wanted to tell the story. We know that many

authors of books for children are Christians, but their starting point is not a lesson and curriculum is not their purpose.

Some of our concern about content is rooted in a rather limited view of Christian education. When we are responsible for planning a church school class or a weekend retreat we have specific goals in mind that direct our choice of resources. Our materials must mesh with our purposes if our education is to be effective. However, learning occurs in many settings other than those we plan as educational events. We learn in worship, in conversations, on occasions of service, around the family table, or in moments of decision about spending money or time.

When a young person says to us, "Tell me some good books to take on vacation," or the mother of a convalescing child calls to ask, "What can we read?" or we collect a box of books for family camp, then we have an unexcelled educational opportunity. When we speak of literature as an essential resource in the church's educational ministry, we have this wider concept in mind.

So—finally—to answer the question "Is children's literature a valid, reliable resource for the church?": Yes. This reading can give us a greater appreciation and understanding of how God has spoken to us, can help us be a stronger community of shared stories, and can widen our view of the world in which our faith is to be lived. We need to realize the nature and limits of literature, but in many instances stories can be the most direct and reliable route to the biblical truth we want to hear.

First, however, read. Read with an open mind and heart. And as you read, for no reason in the world except the reading, we are willing to bet our library cards you will find yourself thinking, "When can I tell this marvelous story?" "That's exactly what I'm trying to say next Sunday." "How can I use this in . . . ?" When you reach that point, you may want to turn to Part IV. But for the moment, simply travel this reliable route. You will find yourself in a different country, a place of unexpected and delightful treasures.

PART II
The Two-way Thoroughfare

Children's literature is not a one-way communication bridge. We must learn from it before we speak through it. We suggest that there are three major reasons for reading children's literature. One is to learn something about children, to understand better what goes on in the mind and heart of a child. Another is to listen to the way children's literature asks and answers life's major questions. Still another is to learn some of the techniques of communication good writers use so effectively. What happens when we listen to the voices from the other side of the bridge—the children and the writers?

4

Connecting Children and Adults

What happens when we read children's literature? How will we change? What effect will it have on the church?

Who can say? Our guess is that we will know a great deal more about children; we might be a bit more sensitive to the needs of the least among us; we might giggle more and have a sense of fun and eagerness that will spill over into our most serious activities.

What can we learn? A lot. Children's books introduce us to a houseful of children who may be observed with leisure and detachment. Children of literature come in all shapes and sizes, with all the feelings, problems, achievements, and needs our own children have, but without the harrowing sense of immediacy that allows no time for contemplation. We can enter their world through their stories, and from these same stories the children can speak to our lives. But let us launch our exploration of the world of children from the solid ground of science.

Although children and adults have a host of common needs and emotions, the ways in which they react and reflect on these vary—or should—with maturity. We have reams of information about how children develop and grow. This science has produced an extensive, documented catalog of childhood behavior and books of resultant theories. In addition, we have another set of careful observations about childhood—those of our storytellers. While it is true that these last observations are intuitive and reportorial, they are uncannily accurate when measured against the discoveries of science.

Children According to Science

We can illustrate by talking about children's growth and development in the middle years, say grades one to seven, or ages six to twelve.

Piaget, whose careful and voluminous work is known world-wide, says that all children go through certain developmental stages *in order*—not always at the same time, but always in the same sequence. The last two cognitive stages of childhood are Stage Four, when children begin to comprehend the workings of the world without understanding the general principles which underlie them, a task that progresses through the middle years; and Stage Five, the final stage, when one begins to grasp logical and abstract principles. So the middle years may be seen as the progression in understanding from *how* to *why* (see Gruber and Vonèche, 1977).

Eric Erikson (1964) does not dispute Piaget, but says in addition that the progress in understanding from *how* the world works to *why* it works as it does demands the development of concurrent abilities such as physical skills, social skills, and the basics of academic attainment. The extent to which these skills are acquired results in the way one copes with life, at this stage either with industry or with inferiority. Erikson sees these two coping methods as opposing solutions. Since in school the child is brought into contact with a wider world of adults, he or she often acquires a perception of incompleteness. Quite clearly, the child is a child and has a great deal to learn. To combat a sense of inferiority, the child needs to develop a sense of industry and determination to succeed in whatever he or she is about.

David Ausubel (1980) sees the middle childhood years as a movement in status for the child. These years are what he calls the time of the satellite personality. The child now has learned that he or she is not the center of the universe. The self-centered, egocentric status has given way to the understanding that the child is dependent on the parents for physical necessities and cannot usually cope with outside relationships without having at least the possibility of running back to the parents for emotional and moral support, sympathy, or encouragement. Still, self-esteem must be preserved, and this can be done only if the parents become the center of the universe, and the child becomes their

15

satellite. The movement from childhood to adulthood is from this derived status to personal primary status; that is, status due to the individual's own competence and attributes. In childhood this status is manifested in areas such as grades, sports, and so forth.

Finally, or maybe initially, for the purpose of this discourse Abraham Maslow (1970) sets up a hierarchy of needs in his theory of motivation and personality, a hierarchy which implies that the most basic human physiological needs such as food, warmth, and sleep quickly give way, once they are satisfied, to higher necessities: the need for love; the need for esteem and self-actualization (the desire to become everything one is capable of becoming); the need to know and understand; and the need for aesthetics. He believes that the development of motivation and personality depends in large part upon the way these needs are met and the values that are placed on them. In other words, he is saying that humans have a higher nature which is part of their essence. His *Motivation and Personality* is fascinating reading.

Children According to Literature

Now we can turn to children, their developmental stages, and their needs, as seen by storytellers.

Perhaps no one understands the American landscape of childhood better than Beverly Cleary. The fears, guilts, trials, and triumphs of growing up seem true both to adults and to children who can put themselves in the place of Henry Huggins and his dog, Ribsy, of Ellen Tebbits, and Ramona Quimby. It is what we would call the safe world of childhood; that is, it is walled by the love and protection of responsible adults.

But the fears and troubles of the larger world outside school and family leak in and demand responses from the children. Ramona first appears as a toddler and grows through successive books. Ramona's father loses his job; Ramona's mother goes to work full-time; both parents suffer disappointments, become tired and cross, and cannot deliver all of their children's expectations. And yet, over and over in all these books, the child's sense of worth is affirmed. Better than almost anyone else, Cleary points out the child's unceasing need for reassurance.

Once is not enough. Daily the child needs to understand that he or she is acceptable. Cleary seems to know what Agatha Bowley wrote in *The Natural Development of the Child:* "Life is something of a battle, not only for the adult with his manifold responsibilities, but also for the child striving to understand his world, to reduce his anxieties, to adjust to the harsh requirements of reality" (1966, 67).

Ramona, whose imagination expands her ordinary world so that she is never sure when she steps from one to the other, knows that deep down inside she is nice. But how is it that so much of what she does is interpreted as naughty or not nice? Ramona is six and in the first grade in *Ramona the Brave*. After Ramona destroys Susan's owl and the teacher talks to the parents, Ramona explains to her mother and father:

> "I wanted my owl to be my very own."
> Of course, you did," said Mr. Quimby, who had once drawn cartoons for his high-school paper. "Every artist wants his work to be his very own, but that does not excuse you from trying to destroy Susan's owl."
> Ramona let out a long shuddering sigh. "I just got mad. Old copycat Susan thought she was so big."
> [Now comes the reassurance.]
> Mrs. Quimby smoothed Ramona's blankets. "Susan is the one I feel sorry for. You are the lucky one. You can think up your own ideas because you have imagination."
> Ramona was silent while she thought this over. "But that doesn't help now," she said at last.
> "Someday it will." Mrs. Quimby rose from the bed. "And Ramona, Mrs. Griggs expects you to apologize to Susan for destroying her owl."
> "Mama!" cried Ramona. "Do I *have* to?"
> "Yes, Ramona, you do." Mrs. Quimby leaned over and kissed Ramona good-night.
> "But, Mama, it isn't fair! Susan is a copycat and a tattletale."
> Mrs. Quimby sighed again. "Maybe so, but that does not give you the right to destroy her property."
> . . . The next morning as Ramona left for school, she asked her mother what she could say to Susan.
> "Just say 'I'm sorry I spoiled your owl,'" said Mrs. Quimby. "And Ramona—try to stay out of mix-ups after this."
> . . . Ramona's feet felt heavy as she walked through soggy leaves. How could she stay out of mix-ups when she never knew what would suddenly turn into a mix-up? She plodded on, as if she were wading through glue . . . (111–14).

Earlier in the book we hear this exchange between Ramona and her older sister:

> "Ramona, grow up!"
> Ramona lost all patience. *"Can't you see I'm trying?"* she yelled at the top of her voice. People were always telling her to grow up. What did they think she was trying to do? (34)

In *Ramona and Her Father*, Ramona is now seven. Her father is out of work; there is tension in the household. Mrs. Quimby looks anxious, either over the cost of groceries or the money the family owes. Ramona's big sister has turned into a regular old grouch.

All this worried Ramona. She wanted her father to smile and joke, her mother to look happy, her sister to be cheerful, and Picky-picky to eat his food, wash his whiskers, and purr the way he used to (63).

Elementary school children grow with Ramona, but they do not lose interest in younger children. They are still close enough to empathize, and yet far enough away to take pride in their own progress and achievement in moving beyond the stage of the character in the book. Astrid Lindgrin of Sweden shows how universal is Cleary's world of childhood, in a book about five-year-old *Lotta on Troublemaker Street.* Lotta grows angry with her mother because she cannot wear her best dress to play in. She cuts a hole in the sweater she has been told to wear and runs away from home to the kind neighbor, Mrs. Berg. (Still safe, you see.) There follows what is essentially a charming exposition of the Prodigal Son. The episode could be read in its entirety and would enchant adults and children alike.

As another example, Maurice Sendak's *Where the Wild Things Are,* a preschool picture book, continues to have fascination for early primary grade children who understand, if only dimly, the fact that Max's wild things are a product of his own nature. They share Max's satisfaction when he has mastered and tamed the wild things. They share his need to return home to love and a good hot supper.

Children's writers seem to know how important it is to children when they master certain skills. Eleanor Estes in *Rufus M.,* Beverly Cleary in the *Ramona* books, and Louise Fitzhugh in *Harriet the Spy* all point out the pride with which their respective characters write their own names. Their names—put by the children themselves on papers and possessions—become tangible evidence of both skill and identity.

Then there are the precocious English children one meets in the novels of Edith Nesbit, C. S. Lewis, L. M. Boston, and Mary Norton, to name a few. These are children who have adventures "on their own." Adults are background necessities to provide food and shelter, but the world is a child's world, where obstacles are met and overcome through the children's own ingenuity. What do these books tell us? Children want to cope, to succeed. Besides that, children learn almost always that there is a cause and effect to events, and that their actions have consequences.

Edward Eager's *Half Magic* is a story with an American setting similar to those stories mentioned above. Often these stories are written with tongue in cheek. They are fun, witty, and rather sophisticated in dialogue and presentation. Eager introduces one of the four children in his book:

Katharine was the middle girl, of docile disposition and a comfort to her mother. She knew she was a comfort, and docile, because she'd heard her mother say so. And the others knew she was, too, by now, because ever since that day Katharine *would* keep boasting about what a comfort she was, and how docile, until Jane declared she would utter a piercing shriek and fall over dead if she heard another word about it. This will give you some idea of what Jane and Katharine were like (3–4).

This is the other side of the coin. While it is important to take seriously the trials and tribulations of childhood, a little perspective, a little humor in viewing oneself, a tolerance for foibles and idiosyncrasies also help children to understand life and how to cope with it.

How the world works and why it works as it does need to be learned both in terms of one's own experience and from points of view that are not one's own. For the Black child the works of Ouida Sebestyen, Mildred Taylor, Rosa Guy, Virginia Hamilton, and Sharon Bell Mathis illustrate the learning, assimilation, and adaptive process that are part of growing up. For the white child, in addition, they convey a perspective and a point of view absolutely necessary in the growth of understanding that the human condition is universal, that love, endurance, and courage cut across racial and cultural lines just as surely as does cruelty. The same may be said for Laurence Yep's stories of Chinese Americans, and for Erik Haugaard's stories of Italian refugees of the second World War.

It is not possible to talk about books that teach adults something about children, and children something about themselves and life, without mentioning Judy Blume, who, according to almost all polls of children themselves, is the most popular writer for children today. She is a controversial writer because she is accused both of shallowness and of a lack of literary finesse and style. It is her subject matter, however, that makes her popular. She seems to know unerringly what the concerns and emotions of the young are like. "I remember my own childhood," she says. *Are You There God? It's Me, Margaret* is a landmark in juvenile literature, dealing as it does with a twelve-year-old and her anxieties about coming menstruation. It was the first time such an issue had been dealt with openly and frankly, and the book opened the gates to a flood of "problem" stories by other authors dealing with everything from child abuse and drug abuse to homosexuality. Her books ought to be read because so many children have read them.

Natalie Babbitt is a writer of another sort. Thoughtful and provocative, she deals with life in another way. She writes of death, immortality, and the meaning of time and space with deftness and great talent. She does this in the context of stories which are exciting and true to the experience of childhood, but removed usually to another era, an unidentified place, so that they seep into the consciousness without the immediacy and urgency of a contemporary story. In *Tuck Everlasting,* when Winnie accidentally discovers the spring of eternal life, she is persuaded by Tuck not to drink it or to divulge its existence. It is because of Tuck's explanation of life and change and death, which is profound and yet simple enough for a child to understand, that Winnie senses she may not wish to be eternal in a finite world.

Just as Ramona in *Ramona the Brave* wants the owl she designed to be hers alone, so Winnie wants to make a contribution that will be unique. Because she has no playmates, she talks to a toad who hops into her fenced-in yard:

> "I'm not exactly sure what I'd do, you know, but something interesting—something that's all mine. Something that would make some kind of difference in the world"(11).

Here it is, as clearly expressed as it can possibly be: the elementary human urge to matter, to find one's own special thing to do. And it starts right away—the progress toward self-actualization.

We saw this process in Ramona; Louise Fitzhugh elaborates on the same theme in *Harriet the Spy* and *Nobody's Family Is Going to Change.* When Harriet finds that her true self is blocked, she undergoes a complete change of personality:

> . . . "I feel different" came slowly into her head. She sat digesting the thought like a Thanksgiving dinner.
>
> Yes, she thought, after a long pause. And then, after more time, Mean, I feel mean.
>
> She looked around with a mean look for everyone. Nobody saw her. She felt her face contorting. It was an impressive moment that everyone missed. It was a moment that Harriet would never forget (225).

Harriet makes two important discoveries. She discovers what happens when she cannot be herself, and she learns she cannot be what she wants to be in a vacuum. She cannot disregard kindness and consideration for others in her own pursuit of self-expression. Friends are important. Her old nurse writes to her:

> Little lies that make people feel better are not bad. . . . Remember, that writing [truth] is to put love in the world, not to use against your friends. But to yourself you must always tell the truth (276).

Partly, it is this advice to tell a necessary lie that makes *Harriet the Spy* one of the most controversial books of its time. It was published in the early sixties. It is, however, an important book and one that is standing the test of time.

The push toward self-actualization is dealt with again by Fitzhugh in *Nobody's Family Is Going to Change.* Emma and Willie learn that they must be what they are called to be in spite of objections and obstacles presented on the part of others—in this case their family. Here are wonderfully exact reproductions of the kind of conversations between parents and children that seem always at cross purposes. Those conversations are as real as if somebody had been outside the door capturing them on a tape recorder.

Bowley points out that in the upper elementary years there is less dependence on parents and more sociability with other children. These years are the time of close friendships, clubs, and elaborate organization within the clubs. Children are not usually very thoughtful of the needs of others; rather, they are almost totally taken up in their own affairs, immersed in their own pursuits which possess a sense of urgency for them. Rockwell's *How to Eat Fried Worms,* Fitzhugh's *Harriet the Spy,* and Estes' *The Hundred Dresses* tell us the same thing.

Despite this self-preoccupation, children have a keen sense of justice, a need for right to prevail. The cognitive task of this age is, according to Piaget's scheme, sometimes designated as "the creation of rules." Bringing order into his world of many discrete facts, the child does not welcome viewpoints and actions that challenge his newly-discovered laws. "That's not fair" is a common cry of the school-age child. Not until the late elementary years does he or she begin to deal with motives as well as actions.

Fairy tales, fantasies, and fables answer this expressed need for justice. Bruno Bettelheim further elaborates on the important function of fairy tales in his book, *The Uses of Enchantment.* Here right prevails, good is rewarded, wrong is punished. Undoubtedly, we as adults should look at these tales again with the eyes of a child to recapture our lost hope and reestablish our visionary capacity.

The matter-of-fact, industrious child of these school years needs and responds to goodness that does not quite fit these black and white categories. When this goodness is seen in realistic fiction, it has a special appeal. In this sense, the heartbreaking and beautiful *Sounder* by William Armstrong is almost a complete education in itself. Firmly grounded in reality, pain, and suffering, the book becomes at the end an ode to the great mystery and beauty of life. What does *Sounder* tell us about children? It tells us that given the basics of trust and respect from adults they admire, children have great capacity for endurance, tenacity in clinging to ideals, ability to adapt, and above all ability to rise above hatred. Paterson's *The Great Gilly Hopkins* repeats this message. Children are tough, but they cannot go it alone.

It seems clear that children sense the tension between the good that should be and the bad that often is. They sense it in their lives, in their own natures, and in the world around them. The books we have mentioned, as well as the fantasy worlds of Lloyd Alexander and Susan Cooper, concretize for children the struggle between good and evil, make tangible the sense of triumph when virtue overcomes, and provide necessary nourishment in the growth of a healthy psyche.

All these examples reveal good literature as a growing place, no matter what age it is intended for. These stories make us appreciate how much children want to understand and grow, to make sense of the world. They also make us appreciate the tremendous responsibility of adults to help children achieve this. Reading these stories, we understand afresh that the terror of the world strikes at the heart of the young as well as the old and that we cannot begin too soon to comprehend and tame our divided natures. We see how literal and concrete are the first steps toward understanding and how necessary are opportunities for experimentation, for forays into independence with the assurance of a safe retreat. We are especially aware of the necessity in children's lives for stretches of free time. But perhaps the overwhelming impression is the insistent demand for a moral, logical world, and the impression that perhaps the logic is of a different order and dimension than we presently grasp. These stories remind us that fiction is not at odds with facts, but that it simply adds another voice and another view to what science records.

What we have tried to do for the elementary years through these books can also be done for preschool children and early adolescents. Viorst's Alexander, Sendak's Max, Heide's Treehorn, Caudill's Charley, and the young Ramona in Cleary's books can open the world of the four- and five-year-old for us, with little text and many pictures. The books containing these characters are all listed in the bibliography. Clearly these books are not written for adults, but they can tell adults something about life and about children. When we read them we are better able to understand the problems of growing up and growing out and reaching for a responsible life in the world.

This literature plants children squarely in the world of childhood where their sense of inadequacy and incompleteness is overcome. It helps children mature toward thoughtfulness and human empathy by creating some perspective from which to view their own immediate activities and goals. And if, as someone has said, "We become ourselves through others," then both children and adults will be encouraged as we read of those who fail, who make mistakes, and yet who are still portrayed as redeemable and worthwhile. We will be spurred on by those who overcome terrible odds, and sweetened by those who refuse to be embittered.

These stories can help us share with our children their task of learning about themselves and can give us points of reference when we seek to impart the Christian faith. The two-way thoroughfare takes us into the lives of children and brings them into our world with voices to tell us where they are and what they need.

5

Connecting
the Christian Faith
and the World

Reading children's literature can help the church speak in a lively, comprehensible way about faith. When we have something to say it will not come out in either gothic print or "in" phrases. We will be less bound by vocabulary, more concerned with idea, more committed to basics, more flexible on peripheral matters, and more comfortable in dialogue with those who stand in a different place. We think that all this is possible because children's literature deals with themes of crucial importance, basic questions we all ask in life, in ways that are clear and vital.

Let us invite our friend Milo and his companions Tock and Humbug to join the conversation once more. Travelling in the Lands Beyond, they approach Digitopolis and are met by the twelve-faced Dodecahedron who delights in problems:

> "I'm not very good at problems," admitted Milo.
> "What a shame," sighed the Dodecahedron. "They're so very useful. Why, did you know that if a beaver two feet long with a tail a foot and a half long can build a dam twelve feet high and six feet wide in two days, all you would need to build Boulder Dam is a beaver sixty-eight feet long with a fifty-one-foot tail?"
> "Where would you find a beaver that big?" grumbled the Humbug. . . .
> "I'm sure I don't know," he replied, "but if you did, you'd certainly know what to do with him."
> "That's absurd," objected Milo. . . .
> "That may be true," he acknowledged, "but it's completely accurate, and as long as the answer is right, who cares if the question is wrong? If you want sense, you'll have to make it yourself" (Juster, 174–175).

Making sense is a primary occupation for humans. We have seen it as a continuous activity in children's development; it persists throughout life. We come to a turning point, a crisis, an unexpected good or tragedy.

We must make a choice, or we differ with our community about what is good and valuable. A natural disaster destroys what has been built on the laws of nature. We face death or, as science prolongs life when thought and meaningful relationships seem ended, we face life. Each situation raises questions: Who are we? Why are we here? Why do we act as we do? How are we related to this vast, mysterious universe? Where are we going? How can we know? How can we be sure? These questions are asked universally.

Literature and Faith
Address Universal Themes

Our faith asks these questions and has something to say about each of them. Phrased in other ways, these concerns form the table of contents of our theological texts. In briefest summary, we find our answers in Jesus Christ.

And here, the Dodecahedron, in the manner of good literature, tells us something about ourselves and perhaps many others like us. We have lived in the context of this answer long before we could actually phrase the question. Many of us learned "Man's chief end is to glorify God and enjoy Him forever" before we learned to read. This order of learning has been a positive blessing, but it has a peculiar danger. We are inclined to be like the students in the math class who settle for the right answer and forget the principle of how the problem is worked. We forget that answers and questions must be connected, that different problems present themselves and thus the answer must be reached once more.

Art, and literature as a form of art, can be most helpful to us, for literature, like theology, addresses these human concerns. One of the sure marks of good literature is the significance of themes or universal questions that emerge through style, plot, and character. In such works we will find still other words and ways to ask about the meaning and purpose of life and other ways to connect our answer with these questions.

We will find these major themes or universal concerns in children's literature no less than in that of adults. Calvino has spoken of Italian folk tales as a general explanation of life. Bruno Bettelheim emphasizes the importance of fairy tales in summarizing the struggle of good and evil and the triumph of justice. We find ideas of equal significance in juvenile fiction written today.

Burch's Queenie Peavy, Sara in Byars' *The Summer of the Swans,* Lena in Sebestyen's *Words by Heart,* and Andy in Krumgold's *Onion John* must all answer the question "Who am I?" through the choices they make. Why are we here? Mary Call in the Cleavers' *Where the Lilies Bloom,* Taran in Alexander's *The Prydain Chronicles,* Forbes' *Johnny Tremain,* and Casey in Yep's *Child of the Owl* ask this question and find clues to the answer. Good and Evil? The fantasies of George MacDonald, C. S. Lewis, and Susan Cooper present this struggle of life in strong, clear strokes. Death? Look at Lewis' *The Last Battle,* Paterson's *Bridge to Terabithia,* White's *Charlotte's Web,* Miles' *Annie and the Old One,* Margaret Brown's *The Dead Bird,* and Babbitt's *Tuck Everlasting.* The search and the vision are present in unnamed lands of fantasy, in rural mountains, in colonial America, in a native American hogan, and in a western town in reconstruction days. Estes' *The Hundred Dresses,* Waldron's *The Integration of Mary-Larkin Thornhill,* and Krumgold's *Henry 3* show the struggle to choose what is good when the community differs. Armstrong's *Sounder,* Mary in the *Little House* series by Wilder, and Green's *Summer of My German Soldier* give us an opportunity to find meaning in suffering.

The list could be expanded. There is no emotion or theme that these books do not touch. This is not to say that Beverly Cleary is a substitute for Jane Austen, that Krumgold's *. . . And Now Miguel* will replace *Great Expectations,* or that adults should give up *War and Peace* for the *Little House* series. But where themes are concerned, books for children provide needed education, for we must speak of profound meanings to listeners of differing ages at different places in life.

As you read with a growing awareness of the questions that enable us to see the relation between our theological questions and humanity's basic questions, you will be disappointed if you look for answers that represent a full-blown Christian theology. You must bring your theology to these books for dialogue and testing as well as for insight and information.

Children's literature has many "Christian" characteristics, especially in its basic hopefulness and recognition of the good and miraculous. It carries a fundamental faith that the world, however muddled, is good.

However, literature, even when it is theological, is not theology and we cannot measure it by textbook standards. We can be open to the parallels between biblical and fictional characters, between ancient and contemporary questions, and between responses, both good and evil, that are present in any age.

For example, four contemporary fictional characters—Andy, Lena, Queenie, and Sara—must make life-determining choices just as Daniel, Peter, and Jacob did in the Bible. These decisions require honesty and courage; they are shaped by heritage and community. Of the four examples, only Lena makes a choice with God's Word as the ultimate reference point. Her story is a simple and moving illustration of what it means to live the words of the Bible and to assume the role of suffering servant. But all of these four characters portray humorously, poignantly, or gently the common needs that call for God's grace and the deep yearning to be more than we are, a longing to which Jesus spoke as he called the disciples and the rich young ruler.

Children's Literature Simplifies Complex Themes

The way universal themes evolve in these works is a lesson in how to approach a complex idea simply, yet without diminishing its significance. At least one strand of the truth is comprehensible to every listener or reader.

Katherine Paterson, comparing the "intricacy, density, design" of an adult novel like Anne Tyler's *Celestial Navigation* with the simplicity of her own *Bridge to Terabithia,* hears in the first a "symphony" and in the latter a "flute solo, unaccompanied." Even in dealing with a most complex historical situation, she says, "I . . . tend to hear through all the storm and clamor a rather simple melody" (1981, 36).

Joseph Krumgold, who like Paterson won the Newbery award twice, describes the effect of writing with children as an audience. Writing "simply and sharply from the child's point of view imposed an altered structure [and] developed a different and a deepened theme" (1967, 2). What had been the film script for a movie about shepherds in New Mexico became a story of confirmation. This distilling and deepening of theme is one blessing that results when we approach a subject through the mind of a child.

. . . And Now Miguel, Onion John, and *Henry 3* by Krumgold are excellent examples of a universal theme emerging through events and choices children understand. Krumgold says that all three of the books are stories of confirmation. They are some of the most fruitful reading a leader of youth or a teacher of a commissioning class can find.

Simplification means less—fewer characters, fewer words, shorter time span, fewer issues. . . . *And Now Miguel* focuses on a single desire. Miguel wants to go with the men when the sheep are taken to the high mountains for the summer. In this situation the summer work identifies one as a man rather than a boy. This is a book on a single issue, a story that reaches a single, satisfying conclusion.

However—and this is the art of good storytellers—that single pebble dropped in the water makes many concentric circles. Miguel is humiliated by a mistake he makes during shearing. It will affect, he fears, his chance to go to the mountains. On a deeper level, how he handles failure will affect his journey to maturity. Miguel prays to go to the mountains. The answer to his prayer pushes him to theological insights that will shape his life. He must make a decision about skipping school to save the family sheep. Again, Miguel and those who approach the story on the simplest level weigh this decision against Miguel's consuming goal. The action is symbolic of all the independent steps that must be taken and weighed against family authority and identity.

Joan Aiken, who writes about writing as skillfully as she writes for children, gives us insight into why children's writers become masters of this sort of multi-layering of ideas. Children read and reread the same books over a period of a decade; therefore a book needs a kind of "quadruple, quintuple richness, so as to be able to take all this extra wear and tear." Her words to note are: ". . . a book ought ideally to have something new to offer them at every reading—a sort of graded series of concepts, graspable at each stage of development" (1976, 20–21). In contrast to many of us who speak to the intergenerational community, writers for children pay careful attention to the aspect of the theme most accessible to the youngest listener, without decreasing the artistic requirements of expression or diluting the thematic content.

Skillfully, the authors choose a single concept or strand and place it within the grasp of a young mind, yet manage not to detach it from the whole. Bridwell's *Clifford,* Laughlin's *The Little Leftover Witch,* Paterson's *The Great Gilly Hopkins,* and Sebestyen's *Words by Heart* deal with love. Each is a true statement, expanding its picture of love and what it does. Emily Elizabeth simply, lovingly accepts Clifford as he is, and we laugh at the results. Trotter in *Gilly Hopkins* does the same thing, but the cost and the implications become clearer. Love is acceptance and discipline in *The Little Leftover Witch;* it is acceptance, discipline, and letting go in *Gilly Hopkins.* In *Words by Heart* love is acceptance, discipline, sacrifice, and losing life to save life.

The single strands in more advanced works are combined into powerful and moving statements about the nature and expression of love, all conveyed through actions and choices. The more complex picture does not sacrifice the single, graspable strand.

Moreover, authors of children's books recognize that themes are grasped in ways not purely intellectual. ". . . . [Children] see only part of the whole, but what they do see is seen truly, is not distorted. Fully understanding a book is too often like being led forward in front of a pointillist painting, and shown how the green is made up of spots of pure blue and pure yellow. One 'understands,' but one can no longer see green" (Walsh 1975, 60).

"Does your book have a theme, or is it meant to be read for pleasure?" wrote a young reader to Joan Aiken (1982, 89). What we learn from the themes of children's literature is that serious theme and pleasure are not mutually exclusive. Sendak's Max, Viorst's Alexander, Cleary's Ramona, Paterson's Gilly, and even Jess in Paterson's tragic *Bridge to Terabithia* all live their stories with humor, without taking themselves too seriously, with an honesty and lack of self-consciousness that make asking questions one of life's most profoundly joyful experiences.

6

Connecting Speaker and Listener

From reading children's literature, we can become a listening as well as a speaking church, seeking not so much to be understood as to understand. We will emphasize "talking with" rather than "talking to." We will rely less on jargon and clichés and instead use fresh and lively words to make abstractions concrete. In short, we will learn something about communication.

There are at least three valuable lessons in communication, and we begin with the hardest, for it rests not in technique or skill but in attitude. Reading these books and listening to their creators talk of their work can show us the basics of communication: a sense of partnership with the reader and a commitment to the truth of the story.

The Foundation of Communication

Communication is by dictionary definition a two-way thoroughfare. Sharing, imparting, partaking, using, enjoying in common, sending messages back and forth, being connected and open to each other—these are some of the ways communication is defined. The writer of good books for children is keenly aware of the contribution the reader makes. Of all who speak of this, perhaps Katherine Paterson says it best in her acceptance speech for the 1981 Newbery medal winner, *Jacob Have I Loved:*

> I have learned, for all my failings and limitations, that when I am willing to give myself away in a book, readers will respond by giving themselves away as well, and the book that I labored over so long becomes in our mutual giving something far richer and more powerful than I could have ever imagined (1981, 125).

Partnership, naturally, is formed by knowing something of the partner—who she is, how he feels, what contributions she can make, what abilities he has. In most instances this knowledge comes from knowing children in the family, for many authors are parents as well. Paterson, Betsy Byars, and Joan Aiken speak of insights gained from their own children. Irene Hunt, a librarian and Newbery winner, relates as a friend to many children.

Not all authors have such personal knowledge of the young. C. S. Lewis, for example, whose Narnia series delights children year after year, evidently had little contact with children. What he did have is that quality referred to by Karl, a link with his own childhood. In fact, the surest bridge to this understanding of the reading partner is built from the recollection of what it was like to be a child. This should be good news to those of us who find it difficult to talk with children. We were, after all, children once.

Eleanor Cameron (1962) has a thought-provoking observation in *The Green and Burning Tree* that touches on the roots of communication. She notes that virtually every successful writer of fantasy for children has lived a childhood touched by sorrow and loneliness, and she cites Lewis, Nesbit, Anderson, Grahame, Kipling, and Thurber as examples. Katherine Paterson, whose work includes realistic historical and contemporary fiction, describes the stress and isolation of returning from China during the war as part of her childhood. We would hope that suffering is not essential for creative communication, but this may be wishful thinking. Having suffered in childhood certainly provides an empathic realization that the young *do* suffer, and not in a superficial way.

A most outstanding example of this ability to recreate childhood experience is in the Wilder *Little House* books. Begin with the first book, *Little House In the Big Woods,* and see the housework and father's homecoming through the eyes of a five-year-old. Then, with each succeeding book, as Laura grows, note how the viewpoint alters slightly. The chapters are filled with physical, tangible details—smells, colors, temperatures, textures—as a growing child would experience them. Listing Wilder's nouns and verbs in a single chapter is a good exercise to stimulate our own childhood memories, though we live in a different century.

Whatever the source—their own children, young friends, or childhood memories—those who communicate well have shared the hopes, fears, needs, joys, problems, pains, and yearning of those with whom they speak; they have maintained the individual flavor of their experiences through active memory; and they have listened as children, for almost all were readers and story-lovers in their early years.

An essential aspect of this partnership is respect, respect for the childhood years as well as for the children. We see it in disciplined craftsmanship, in choice of significant themes, in a refusal to talk down to or manipulate the reader. Authors speak with special vehemence against condescension, coyness, and "writing down" to a presumably inferior audience.

Respect is shown in asking something of the audience. Hard words and profound questions are served up without apology. There is an open, unfinished aspect to these books where pictures must be filled in, conclusions must be drawn, and new visions must be followed. Edward Ardizzone, a prize-winning illustrator, says that the best picture of a hero is his back as he is walking away. The face is the reader's responsibility. Joan Aiken wants her readers to go back and puzzle. Helen Cresswell describes her books as journeys and explorations, suggesting that destination and discovery lie with the reader.

There is a high level of trust between writer and reader. We suspect that no one can address another with meaning in the absence of this trust and respect. When age, authority, achievement, skill, or education makes us feel superior and more powerful, then we lose this sense of partnership. Trust, respect, and partnership are embedded in the words and works of writers for children.

The authors of children's literature have an equal respect for the story they tell. The second dominant theme we find when writers talk about their work is commitment to the truth of the story. Let us clarify this, however, with two negative comments. This does not mean telling about a historically verifiable event in a factual, journalistic style. It does not mean uncensored expression of every thought and feeling, nor does it give a higher honesty rating to whatever is sordid, brutal, or generally unpleasant.

Meticulous accuracy where facts are concerned is one evidence of this respect. George's *Julie of the Wolves*, the Collins' *My Brother Sam Is Dead*, and Nesbit's *Five Children and It* are bona fide educations in nature and history. Even though the last mentioned is a fantasy, it is a painless way to learn about ancient Egyptian life. The Cleavers' *Where the Lilies Bloom* is an excellent resource for facts about wildcrafting in the Smokies.

Honesty, in this body of work, means facing consequences—both good and bad—that are inherent in the story. There are no false escapes or manufactured happy endings. Nor are there manufactured morals. Good books have no axes to grind. Nevertheless, with integrity, these works are always both hopeful and profoundly moral.

What comes through in all of this is a picture of the writer as servant rather than possessor of the story. Without using the term "servant," those who tell stories to children—true stories, that is—speak of commitment, of following where the story leads, of obeying the story's form.

Those of us who have a true Story to tell need frequent reminders of these two ideas. Both of them are echoed and re-echoed in books about preaching and teaching. J. Randall Nichols includes a wise and witty "Bill of Rights for Congregations" (1980, 158) in *Building the Word*. It solicits respect for and attention to listeners, and insists that preachers ask for and expect a contribution from congregations. When Fred Craddock writes of inductive preaching in *As One Without Authority* (1979), the listener is center stage; he or she completes the sermon. Thomas H. Groome introduces his seminal *Christian Religious Education* (1980) with the story of how he came to include his students as teaching partners in a high school religion class.

No, these are not original ideas, but they are seldom-practiced ones. We are torn too frequently between loyalty to listener and loyalty to story. We see this in the continuing debate between those who want to begin with the Bible in teaching and those who want to begin where the students are. It is a division which seems to say we must depreciate one or the other. Good books for children are the most consistent demonstration of how to maintain both a sense of story and a sense of audience. And they keep before us the partners in communication most likely to be ignored: children.

First Steps in Communication

It is all very well to talk about attitudes, but communication has to start somewhere. What is the first word? How do writers initiate communication? How is the invitation to partnership issued?

An obvious answer to questions about initiating interest would be "Start with something that interests the reader," but that leaves us with a list too long to be of practical value. We have already spoken of how many subject areas appeal to child and adult alike. So we are looking for answers that tell us "how" rather than "what." We have found at least one of four surefire popular characteristics on the initial pages of every book children begin to read with zest.

One certain success is the story that begins with a question, a dissonance, a situation that creates an immediate need for more information. The question is not necessarily verbalized, though it can be. The elements in the situation may be so incongruous that they arrest our attention. Take, for example, an ax at the family breakfast table.

"Where's Papa going with that ax?" is the opening sentence of White's *Charlotte's Web,* asked by Fern as she is setting the table for breakfast. Something is slightly askew, and we move closer, feeling an urge akin to the desire to straighten a crooked picture or uneven tablecloth.

Or consider the first paragraphs in Barbara Robinson's *The Best Christmas Pageant Ever.* The season of peace and good will is introduced with these words:

The Herdmans were absolutely the worst kids in the history of the world. They lied and stole and smoked cigars (even the girls) and talked dirty and hit little kids and cussed their teachers and took the name of the Lord in vain and set fire to Fred Shoemaker's old broken-down toolhouse.

The toolhouse burned right down to the ground, and I think that surprised the Herdmans. They set fire to things all the time, but that was the first time they managed to burn down a whole building (1).

The superlative Christmas pageant is somehow related to a motley crew of juvenile arsonists, inept ones at that. And while we are with the Herdmans, we can notice that the whole family has been described with nine verbs and one adjective. Excessive modifiers are no failing of Barbara Robinson. Since adults have adopted this book with an enthusiasm equal to that of its young readers, perhaps they too appreciate description through action.

Another early attention-catcher is an emotion, a major ingredient that distinguishes literature from mere information. The angry fear is almost visible on the first page of Byars' *The House of Wings* as Sammy crouches beside the metal culvert, dreading his grandfather's approach, and dreading equally being alone on a busy highway if he is not found.

Even so slight a plot as that in Viorst's *Alexander and the Terrible, Horrible, No Good, Very Bad Day* becomes a compelling story because of Alexander's feelings of absolute frustration and defeat: "I went to sleep with gum in my mouth and now there's gum in my hair and when I got out of bed this morning I tripped on the skateboard and . . ."

A third way of instant involvement is the creation of a place, a specific country or era.

L. M. Boston establishes such a world for the gorilla, Hanno, in *A Stranger at Green Knowe:*

Imagine a tropical forest so vast that you could roam in it all your life without ever finding out there was anything else. Imagine it so dense that even if a man flew over it for hours, his airplane bumping on the rolling uplifts of heat, he would see nothing but the tops of trees from horizon to horizon. It is in such a forest—in the Congo—that this story must begin.

To look for the hero of the story, you must venture into the haunted gloom . . . (9).

The first paragraphs of Wilder's *Little House on the Prairie,* Baum's *The Wizard of Oz,* Tolkien's *The Hobbit,* and Forbes' *Johnny Tremain* sketch scenes so real that we step into their boundaries without conscious choice. We are there before we have time to plan or think.

A fourth way authors engage readers is through a point of contact or a familiar doorway. The reader says, "I've done that. I know how that feels. I'm in this story." We will travel into the different and unknown experience by a known path. There are recognizable signposts to a new destination.

Edith Nesbit anchors her time fantasy, *Five Children and It,* with the very familiar question from the children in the carriage, "Are we there yet?" Claudia Lewis, author and teacher, points out how many stories begin with a journey, a common experience for most of us. Arrivals and departures have about them an uncertainty, an unknown quality, an anticipation known to most children. It is interesting here to think about how many Bible stories deal with journeys. Abraham, Jacob, Joseph, and Moses all traveled to uncertain destinations. But we adults often tell our stories as if we already know the date and hour of arrival.

Another point of contact is established by Miguel, a boy caught in the limbo between childhood and manhood:

I am Miguel. For most people it does not make so much difference that I am Miguel. But for me, often, it is a very great trouble.

It would be different if I were Pedro. He is my younger brother, only seven years old. For Pedro everything is simple. Almost all the things that Pedro wants he has—without much worry (1).

The uncertainty of children in the absence of known authority is a familiar doorway. "Sally and I did not know what to say" (8) when Dr. Seuss' *The Cat in the Hat* invaded the house, presenting a counter authority by sheer energy and force of personality. How familiar is this difficulty to the child who lives under parental rule but must travel into realms where what was clear in one situation is hazy in another! And what a happy chance to see authority defied without one's conscious choice or deliberate cooperation!

Questions, feelings, places, points of contact—these are like personal invitations spoken to a known audience. They are used to initiate communication, to invite the participation of the hearer. They are significant clues to those of us who preach or plan educational experiences. We, like writers, have responsibilities for questions, setting, emotional tones, and points of contact. The arresting incongruity, the environment that woos entry, the feelings that involve, and the familiar signposts issue invitations to any age.

Continuing Communication

How can we maintain communication? Once the listener is involved with us, can we guarantee that he or she will keep on listening? What can we do to maintain the partnership?

Children close the book after the first few pages if there are lengthy passages of introspection, a multitude of flowery adjectives, a protagonist who does nothing, an ax to grind, or unrelieved despair. They stay with action, emotion, surprises, humor, vivid details, and, surprisingly, since we are speaking of printed as well as oral stories—rhythm.

While these observations may help us select interest-sustaining stories, they do not translate neatly into rules for our own speech in communicating. Our most profitable course of action will be to observe how authors use words, the tools of communication, to make characters vivid, plot progressive, settings visible, and abstractions concrete. Select a book from the bibliography that is a Newbery or Carnegie winner and observe as you read.

The Use of Nouns and Verbs

Nouns and verbs—solid, working words—predominate; there are a few, well-chosen modifiers. We have already noted Robinson's description of the Herdmans through verbs. We meet people and even objects through what they do and say.

Mary Call in *Where the Lilies Bloom,* for example, describes the water that she gives the traveler from her family's spring as "pure and so cold it made him clench his teeth" (Cleaver and Cleaver, 7).

We meet Morris the Florist in Merrill's *The Pushcart War* through his sales policy and conversation:

At the time of the Pushcart War, Morris the Florist had been in the flower line for forty-three years . . . . and his only claim to fame before the war was that it was impossible to buy a dozen flowers from him.

If a customer asked Morris for a dozen tulips—or daffodils or mixed snapdragons—Morris always wrapped up thirteen flowers. The one extra was at no cost. "So it shouldn't be a small dozen," Morris said (20).

Miguel describes his first sight of the Sangre de Cristo mountains. The awe and wonder are akin to worship, yet the description is through nouns and sensory experiences:

There was no more Miguel. Only a pair of eyes to look at the green, the great trees of pine and oak. Two eyes, and one nose to pull, like a lamb nursing, at how clean it was and sharp, to smell the chill that was here and the faraway, soft taste of the pine and the spruce. I stood there, no longer me, only a pair of eyes and a nose and two feet that had taken their first step into the Mountains of the Sangre de Cristo (Krumgold, 235–36).

A Rich Vocabulary

Observe, too, the richness of vocabulary. Good writing for children does not depend on easy words, but appropriate words; not short words, but clear and precise words. Natalie Babbitt suggests that we compare the opening words of *A Farewell to Arms* with those of Kipling's "How the Rhinoceros Got His Skin" (157). To sample vocabulary in books for children, read some of Father Rabbit's conversation in Lawson's *Rabbit Hill,* or the tales of Beatrix Potter.

Imagery and Analogies

Some writers succeed with similes, metaphors, and imagery; some succeed without them. We learn by observing and asking why. The pictures may be quick and sharp. Lena thinks of herself ". . . oozing like dark dough over the edges of her last-year's Sunday dress" (Sebestyen 1979, 5). Intelligent, sophisticated Winston speaks of Thursday as "a particular wart in my week" because he must stay with his handicapped sister (Konigsberg 1976, 4).

In Wilder's *Little House on the Prairie* Laura sees a vast picture and the words give us her perspective:

Day after day they traveled in Kansas, and saw nothing but the rippling grass and the enormous sky. In a perfect circle the sky curved down to the level land, and the wagon was in the circle's exact middle (13).

Sometimes the imagery is extended. Henry 3, in Krumgold's book by that name, is a brilliant thirteen-year-old boy who compares losing to a color, a texture, a smell. In trying to tell his mother what the friendship of Fletcher Larkin has meant to him, he compares his friend to the hurricane that had drawn the courageous best out of the community where they live:

"It's as if there were a hurricane every day or maybe a war here in Crestview but with no winds, Ma, and no bombs. It's just as honest one day with him as it is the next. The thing is, with Larkin you don't have to wait until it's dangerous, to do your best. You're always trying" (244).

Sentence Structure

Comprehension is highest for adults and children when subject and predicate are close together. This is the most frequent pattern, especially in books for younger children. Varied lengths—short phrases and long, flowing lines—give variety, texture, and pace. Again, the sentence serves the subject. Henry 3, who narrates his own story, uses a one-sentence paragraph to describe an atomic explosion he sees on television, with phrase growing out of phrase. Andy, on the other hand, is a typical boy in a small community. He expresses his idea of a perfect day in shorter, clipped phrases (see Krumgold's *Onion John*).

Sound and Rhythm

Closely related to sentence structure is the rhythm of sound. Some stories demand to be spoken: "The great, grey-green, greasy Limpopo River" (Kipling 1912, 65), or "hundreds of cats, thousands of cats, millions and billions and trillions of cats" (Gág [1928] 1956), or the schoolroom "sheeted and shrouded and filled with junk . . ." (Norton 1953, 9). Tolkien in *The Hobbit* makes sound a servant of his story; alliteration and onomatopoeia make Bilbo Baggins, the Desolation of Smaug, and Gollum unforgettable to the reader. Thurber's fairy tales sing even when they are read silently. Helen Cresswell's description of the Bongleweed's growth (Ch. 5) is another dazzling example.

Style

The combination of the words, sounds, sentences, and images that bring the story to life is labeled "style." Style is the essence of the story, a collection of a number of elements that, not separately, but in their own peculiar combination, become something alive and original. Style is the idea clothed in garments individually cut and shaped. In children's literature the garments are cut to fit the child.

When style is good, there is room in the garment to move around, to stretch. In *Dragonwings* Laurence Yep describes a mother teaching her son to fly a kite. "She told me then how the string in my hand was like a leash and the kite was like a hound I had sent hunting, to flush a sunbeam or a stray phoenix out of the clouds" (4).

Although this is a fairly long sentence, each part is a logical extension of what went before. Look for a moment at what the sentence accomplishes. A leash on a dog is a familiar image; one understands the pull and tug. Dogs hunting is also familiar, but here is a little stretch. Then comes a strange verb, "flush," and two more images. A sunbeam? Yes, a child knows what that is, but used in this way as if it were a quarry? And "stray phoenix"? Surely, for most children this is new, and the child may not stop, probably will not stop, to find out what a phoenix is. The story is too engrossing not to move on. But several things have happened. First of all, a kind of excitement has been communicated. Secondly, the unfamiliar has followed the familiar in such a way that the context serves to explain and extend understanding. There is still more to learn. Not everything is perfectly understood, but the message is clear and the mind is tugged, like the kite, a little higher.

Let us look at one more example of style, one that is simple, spare, direct and yet evocative, alive, and value-laden. In White's *Charlotte's Web* the life of Wilbur the Pig has been spared because of the written words Charlotte spun over his pen at the fair. Now Wilbur lives out his days in security and gratitude:

Mr. Zuckerman took fine care of Wilbur all the rest of his days, and the pig was often visited by friends and admirers, for nobody ever forgot the year of his triumph and the miracle of the web. Life in the barn was very good—night and day, winter and summer, spring and fall, dull days and bright days. It was the best place to be, thought Wilbur, this warm delicious cellar, with the garrulous geese, the changing seasons, the heat of the sun, the passage of swallows, the nearness of rats, the sameness of sheep, the love of spiders, the smell of manure, and the glory of everything.

Wilbur never forgot Charlotte. Although he loved her children and grandchildren dearly, none of the new spiders ever quite took her place in his heart. She was in a class by herself. It is not often that someone comes along who is a true friend and a good writer. Charlotte was both (183–4).

The Roots of Communication

Good communicators—whether authors for adults, for children, whether teachers or preachers—agree on one fact: sensing comes before expressing. Cameron quotes Flannery O'Connor: "The key word is *see*." Cameron also marshals Joseph Conrad and Gerard Manley Hopkins to support the point (Cameron 1962, 148). These three writers for an adult audience emphasize what Laura Ingalls Wilder practiced so well. One key to her clear and lively writing is that she saw everything twice—once for herself and then verbally for her blind sister. Claudia Lewis, a children's writer and teacher of writers, encourages her students to see and sense in retrospect: "Try to feel out the ingredients of this atmosphere with more than your eyes. Stand there, listen, breathe, take your sweater off, and feel the air of the place on your bare arms, on your neck, your forehead . . ." (Claudia Lewis 1981, 39).

Even Fred B. Craddock, the homiletics professor, emphasizes the value of sensing: "Preaching begins not with expression, but with impression. This calls for a sensitivity to the sights, sounds, and flavors of life about him that is not easily maintained by the minister, or by anyone else" (1979, 80).

Children, we suggest, are better at sensing than are adults, and those who write for children know the necessity of communicating through these sensory impressions. Here is one more good reason that Christians who have something to say should read children's literature.

PART III
Practical Approaches

In this section we want to take you as quickly and smoothly as possible to the books that form the bridge of communication. We will point the way to discerning reading and sources of up-to-date information. We shall also take you into the life of the church where you can help others become familiar with these books. We will give ideas for using literature in ways that will enrich the life of the congregation but require little or no effort. Finally, we will present some designs for using literature in planned education.

7

The Signposts

A wag once remarked, when looking at a series of photographs that contained some by Ansel Adams and others by a rank amateur using a polaroid, "Some are better than others." The same can be said of the over forty thousand children's books in print, and unlike photographs, these books do not reveal their differences at first glance. So where do you start?

Selecting First Books to Read

It is important to begin with a guide to lead you through the maze of titles and authors that confront you as you enter a book store or the children's department of the library. Our favorite guidebook is *Choosing Books for Children* by Betsy Hearne. Other excellent resources are *A Parent's Guide to Children's Reading* by Nancy Larrick, and Kimmel and Segel's *For Reading Out Loud!* You could start reading with any title they suggest.

Guidance is also available through the awards and prizes that are given each year in the field of children's literature. There are at least two sources where you can find this information. The Children's Book Council publishes *Children's Books: Awards and Prizes*, which gives a brief description of each award, the criteria for selection, and a retrospective list of winners. Jones' *Children's Literature Awards and Winners: A Directory of Prizes, Authors, and Illustrators* is basically the same thing, but it is much more comprehensive because it includes a list of award-winning authors and illustrators and their works. If you do not find either of these in your library, the Children's Book Council *Awards and Prizes* is an inexpensive paperback. (See Ch. 13 for ordering address.) Begin with any book included in these lists.

If you are really serious about a systematic overview of what the "experts" consider to be best, a kind of canon, perhaps you should see *Building a Children's Literature Collection* by Quimby and Kimmel. For such

a comprehensive list, it is relatively short. The latest and third edition (1983) lists approximately fifteen hundred titles, both fiction and nonfiction, recommended for a beginning collection to back up the teaching of children's literature. The titles are carefully chosen from thirteen basic sources, all revised or updated in the last five years. Each title in the list appears in at least three original sources. That is to say, the *Choice* list is a synthesis of titles that appear in such aids as *The Children's Catalogue,* Sutherland, Monson, and Arbuthnot's *Children and Books,* and Huck's *Children's Literature in the Elementary School.* Once again, this last is an inexpensive list published in paperback.

At this point, you might be throwing up your hands and saying, "Good heavens," (reverently, of course) "I can't read all of that. Even if I had plenty of interest, I don't have the time." So we will pretend that though you are an adult who has read at least a few children's books since adulthood, you have not read many and you want a short list. We suggest that you start with these eleven books:

(1) *Little Women* by Louisa May Alcott
(2) *The Wonderful Wizard of Oz* by Frank Baum
(3) *Johnny Tremain* by Esther Forbes
(4) *Julie of the Wolves* by Jean C. George
(5) *Island of the Blue Dolphins* by Scott O'Dell
(6) *Where the Wild Things Are* by Maurice Sendak
(7) *The Adventures of Huckleberry Finn* by Mark Twain [Samuel Clemens]
(8) *The Adventures of Tom Sawyer* by Mark Twain [Samuel Clemens]
(9) *Charlotte's Web* by E. B. White
(10) *Little House in the Big Woods* by Laura Ingalls Wilder
(11) *Little House on the Prairie* by Laura Ingalls Wilder

These books were chosen during the 1976 bicentennial by the American Library Association and a group of educators as the outstanding books for children by American authors published in the last two hundred years. By almost anyone's standards, these are great books.

Children's tastes, however, are eclectic, and some of the books children like best do not always measure up to the highest literary standards. They like a book because, for one reason or another, the story stirs a response that excites their imagination, meets a need, or helps them grow. We can think of several such books—*The Boxcar Children* by Gertrude C. Warner, *Where the Red Fern Grows* by Wilson Rawls, and Blume's *Tales of a Fourth Grade Nothing* and *Superfudge*. An annual publication, *Children's Choices,* lists children's selections from books published in the U.S. during the previous year. At least ten thousand children in this country are involved in the selection each year of between 100 and 175 books.

Now you have a starting place from which to talk to children or adults about children's books. It might be interesting at this time to search your memory and list those books you read as a child that you still remember. What made them memorable?

Finally, at the end of this chapter there is an annotated list called "Enduring Favorites: Titles That Have Stood the Test of Time." See how many of these thirty-three titles you know.

Learning to Evaluate Books

How can you tell if a children's book is good? That is a question we are often asked. There is much to be said about critical evaluation—about plot, theme, characterization, style, and form. Rebecca J. Lukens' excellent paperback, *A Critical Handbook of Children's Literature,* discusses these elements in detail. But for a simple answer to a complex question we like Betsy Hearne's statement from *Choosing Books for Children:*

> ". . . The answer to that question of how to tell a good children's book from a bad one is the same as telling a good recipe from a bad one. You just taste it.
>
> Looking and reading are the test. With a little time and interest, anyone can be a first-class, four-star, triple-A children's book connoisseur, and glad of the experience" (25).

Read, read, read. The literature itself sets standards. The more you read and have read, the more you will have to measure against and compare. The book you thought so good the first time you read it may pale in comparison to others you read later.

Of course, certain components of a book may be quite good and others less so. The story can move along at a lively clip (as Nancy Drew books do) and yet be extremely weak in characterization and realistic consequences.

Evaluating a book is like appreciating a piece of weaving. Many strands must be woven into a whole piece to make something more valuable by far than separate spindles of thread, no matter how gloriously colored each may be. To carry the analogy further, once you know which strands go into a piece, if you notice that one is weak or a color is missing, you come to devalue the whole. It is that process of first seeing the whole, then analyzing the components, and finally putting them back together again, that develops the critical sense.

For example, good weaving must exhibit skill in the technical use of the loom, good color sense, original design. In the same way, good books possess to a fine degree one or more of the following components: outstanding theme, clever plot, beautiful language, memorable characters, and so on. Occasionally, though, we encounter a piece of fabric, or a literary vision of life, combining all of the necessary elements with such finesse and style that we can say enthusiastically, "This is a great work of art." Our critical sense tells us that there are many good products—very few great ones.

Then there is the child. When evaluating a children's book, you have a child looking over your shoulder—the child you once were. There are others as well: the children you have known, the children that are yet to be. They are waiting to read what is written about them. They are waiting for the stories that verify their experiences.

At this point the process becomes a paradox. We read children's books to learn again what childhood is like. We judge children's books from the vantage point of an adult, hoping we can become like children once more. And we measure the success of a book to the extent that we feel the sweet sharpness of childhood. But we must never measure a children's book as if it were written by a child. The child must be given the benefit of the perspective and wisdom of the adult. The skill with which this is done without preaching or didacticism is a crucial test of the author's craftsmanship, another strand in the overall worth of the book.

Evaluating Picture Books

Many books for children are picture books. How can you tell when one of these is good? The same strands that combine to produce good fiction are present in a picture book, which usually tells a shorter, simpler story with a single situation and theme. The limited text and the illustrations guarantee that a picture book has something to offer the very young, whose attention span is short. (Do not interpret adaptation to the young as exclusion of adults. See Yashima's *Crow Boy,* for example.) Still, we judge a picture book as we judge any book, with some additional considerations.

The illustrations should be an integral part of the story; without them the story would be incomplete. In a good picture book the pictures actually tell part of the story. Sometimes there are no words at all, and the story is told completely through the illustrations. Peter Spier's *Noah's Ark* is an example. Most of the time, however, the text is necessary to the pictures and the pictures expand the text, creating mood, depicting character, authenticating setting, and in some cases showing action not mentioned in the text. One cannot imagine Sendak's *Where the Wild Things Are* or Heide's *The Shrinking of Treehorn* without illustrations, or vice versa.

We should note here that pictures can tell an additional story, expressing ideas quite apart from the words. The pictures may give details about gender, culture, race, and attitudes. For instance, they may show that only certain work is appropriate for women, that certain roles are filled by one race, that certain conditions exist in a particular culture—all without one word on the subject. Therefore, we evaluate the content of pictures for any separate story that is being told.

The illustrations must also be accurate. Remember that our children are literal-minded. If the text says there are red balloons, they had better be red. If we are told there are nine kittens, a child will count to see if there really are. If the story has a setting geographically and historically realistic, the illustrator should try to recreate the setting and era with fidelity, even though the young may not be able to recognize inaccuracies. (For an example, see Turkle's books about Obadiah.) The pictures should make the book's words credible.

Picture books may be the child's first exposure to visual art. Children's book illustration has called upon the talents of our finest artists, and the wide range of method and media can provide an unconscious lesson in art education and appreciation. Therefore, we must judge the quality of the art—the use of color and line, the composition, the vitality of the whole. The format is another matter of concern; it includes page layouts, typeface, spacing, and quality of the art reproduction.

Remember that experts judge both picture books and longer books. Looking at the winners of the Caldecott awards through the years will help you develop judgment. A book like Cianciolo's *Picture Books for Children* will sharpen your visual awareness.

Keeping Up with Books

How can you keep up with the good children's books published each year? If you become a children's book reader you will eventually ask this question, for there are close to three thousand new titles published each year. Here are four or five rather simple activities that, pursued systematically, will help to keep you abreast.

Know the People Who Work with Books

Get to know the children's librarian in your public library, and/or school media specialists. Do not worry about being bothersome; librarians love to share their information and talk about new books. Every situation varies, of course, but if you express an interest in keeping up with what is new, most librarians will go out of their way to help you. Many receive review copies of new books and would be willing to show them to you.

Most libraries subscribe to several professional reviewing tools. If you do not find them on the shelves for the general public, just ask, and the librarian will probably be delighted to let you see them. *Booklist* is our first choice, folowed by *The School Library Journal* staff reviews. *Publishers Weekly* alerts you to the new titles coming up.

If you volunteer to help in the school library or public library, you will have the advantages of processing or shelving new books, knowing what review helps are available, and claiming the librarian as your friend.

Browse

Lots of children's reading rooms highlight new books in a special place for a short time. Do not forget your bookstores and the people who work there; they also provide suggestions and information. Do not neglect the paperback section, either, since much that is good finally comes out in this form.

Read in Newspapers and Magazines

Read about new books in the popular media. Many newspapers and magazines review children's books on a regular basis. Once you sensitize yourself and learn what to watch for, it is easy to pay attention. Your local newspaper probably has a seasonal review, if not a weekly or monthly column.

Rely on Professional Reports

There are a number of annual lists, compiled by committees of professionals who spend many more hours reading and selecting than you can. The New York Public Library publishes an annual booklet called *Children's Books.* The Association of Library Service to Children (ALSC) of the American Library Association puts out a yearly list called *Notable Books for Children.* *Horn Book Magazine,* too, has an annual Honor List. The Children's Literature Center of the Library of Congress offers a periodic collection of addenda to their main publication, *The Best of Children's Books.* Every

December *The School Library Journal* publishes a list called *Best Books of the Year*.

Try the Interlibrary Loan

Your state library is another resource. If your local public library or bookstore does not have a title you want, most states have an extensive interlibrary loan network through their state libraries. The best way to get details about this is to ask at the circulation or reference desk of your public library. Lacking a public library, you may write to your state library.

Now that you know how to begin—happy reading! Read the best, read what you can get your hands on, read the latest. Be aggressive about finding a particular title you want, then share your enthusiasm and your new discoveries. The first thing you know, you will be part of a reading church!

Enduring Favorites: Titles That Have Stood the Test of Time

These are books that have stood the test of time. They are not included in the main bibliography, partly because they are more apt to be known by adults already, and partly because we have not relied heavily on these for illustrative material. There are several editions of most of these classics, and you can find many picture books based on a single story from any of these collections. We have tried to list complete collections, and good and current editions.

Fairy Tales

Andersen, Hans Christian. *Eighty Fairy Tales*. Trans. by R. P. Keigwin. New York: Pantheon, 1982. 483 pp.

Grimm, Brothers. *The Juniper Tree, and Other Tales from Grimm*. 2 vols. Trans. by Lore Segal and Randall Jarrell. Illus. by Maurice Sendak. New York: Farrar, Straus, Giroux, 1973. 332 pp. Boxed set.

Jacobs, Joseph. *English Fairy Tales*. 3rd ed. Illus. by John D. Batten. New York: Dover, 1967. 261 pp.

Lang, Andrew. *The Red Fairy Book*. Ed. by Brian Alderson. Illus. by Faith Jacques. New York: Viking, 1978. This is perhaps the most popular of the color fairy books—*Green, Yellow, Brown, Grey, Violet, Pink,* and *Olive*. Lang refused to censor any of the stories he gathered from around the world. He insisted that such fare, with all its magic and grisly aspects, helped develop the imagination of children.

Perrault, Charles. *Perrault's Complete Fairy Tales*. Trans. by A. E. Johnson and others. Illus. by

W. Heath Robinson. New York: Dodd, Mead, 1982. 184 pp.

Rackham, Arthur. *The Arthur Rackham Fairy Book: A Book of Old Favourites with New Illustrations*. Illus. by author. Philadelphia: J. B. Lippincott, n.d. 286 pp.

Folk Tales

Aardema, Verna. *Behind the Back of the Mountain: Black Folktales from Southern Africa*. Illus. by Leo and Diane Dillon. New York: Dial, 1973, 85 pp.

Aesop's Fables. Illus. by Heidi Holder. New York: Viking, 1981. 25 pp.

Asbjornsen, Peter Christen. *East of the Sun and West of the Moon: Old Tales from the North*. Illus. by Kay Nielsen. Garden City, NY: Doubleday, 1976. 108 pp.

Chase, Richard, comp. *The Jack Tales*. Appendix compiled by Herbert Halpert. Illus. by Berkeley Williams, Jr. Boston: Houghton Mifflin, 1971. 202 pp. American folk tales from the Carolina mountains.

Harris, Joel C. *Complete Tales of Uncle Remus*. Ed. by Richard Chase. Illus. by Arthur Burdette Frost and others. Boston: Houghton Mifflin, 1955.

Myths and Legends

Aulaire, Ingri d' and Edgar Parin. *Norse Gods and Giants*. Garden City, NY: Doubleday, 1967. 154 pp.

Colum, Padraic. *The Golden Fleece and the Heroes Who Lived Before Achilles*. Illus. by Willy Pogany. New York: Macmillan, 1983. 330 pp.

Hawthorne, Nathaniel. *A Wonder-book and Tanglewood Tales*. Boston: Houghton Mifflin, 1951. 421 pp.

Pyle, Howard. *Some Merry Adventures of Robin Hood, of Great Renown in Nottinghamshire*. Illus. by author. New York: Charles Scribner's Sons, 1976. 212 pp.

———. *The Story of King Arthur and His Knights*. Illus. by author. New York: Charles Scribner's Sons, 1984. 312 pp.

Original Tales That Have Become Classics

Alcott, Louisa May. *Little Women*. Illus. by Tasha Tudor. New York: World, 1969. 544 pp.

Barrie, J. M. *Peter Pan*. Illus. by Trina Schart Hyman. New York: Charles Scribner's Sons, 1980. 184 pp.

Baum, Frank. *The Wizard of Oz*. Illus. by Evelyn Copelman, et al. New York: Putnam, 1956.

Burnett, Frances Hodgson. *The Secret Garden*. Illus. by Tasha Tudor. New York: J. B. Lippincott, 1962.

Carroll, Lewis. *Alice in Wonderland and Through the Looking-Glass*. Illus. by John Tenniel. New York: G. P. Putnam's Sons, 1963. unp.

Collodi, C. [pseud.]. *The Adventures of Pinnochio: Tale of a Puppet*. Trans. by M. L. Rosenthal. Illus. by Troy Howell. New York: Lothrop, Lee, Shepard, 1983. 254 pp.

Milne, A. A. *Winnie-the-Pooh*. Illus. by Ernest H. Shepard. New York: E. P. Dutton, 1961. 161 pp.

———. *The House at Pooh Corner*. Illus. by Ernest H. Shepard. New York: E. P. Dutton, 1961. 180 pp.

Nesbit, E. *The Story of the Amulet*. Illus. by H. R. Miller. New York: Penguin, 1959. 228 pp.

Spyri, Johanna. *Heidi*. Illus. by William Sharp. New York: G. P. Putnam's Sons, n.d. unp.

Stevenson, Robert Louis. *Treasure Island*. Illus. by N. C. Wyeth. New York: Charles Scribner's Sons, 1981. 251 pp.

Twain, Mark [Samuel Clemens]. *The Adventures of Huckleberry Finn* [1885]. Afterword by Alfred Kazin. Bantam Classic ed. New York: Bantam, 1981.

———. *The Adventures of Tom Sawyer*. Illus. by Richard M. Powers. Garden City, NY: Doubleday, 1954.

Verse

Brooke, L. Leslie. *Johnny Crow's Garden: A Picture Book*. Illus. by author. New York: Warne, Frederick, 1903. unp.

De La Mare, Walter, ed. *Come Hither: A Collection of Rhymes and Poems for the Young of All Ages*. Illus. by Warren Chappell. New York: Knopf, 1957. 777 pp.

———. *Rhymes and Verses: Collected Poems for Young People*. Illus. by Elinore Blaisdell. New York: Holt, Rinehart and Winston, 1947. 344 pp.

Lear, Edward. *The Complete Nonsense of Edward Lear*. Ed. by Holbrook Jackson. London: Faber and Faber, 1947. 288 pp.

McCord, David. *One at a Time*. Illus. by Henry B. Kane. Boston: Little, Brown, 1977. 494 pp.

Milne, A. A. *Now We Are Six*. Illus. by Ernest H. Shepard. New York: E. P. Dutton, 1961. 104 pp.

———. *When We Were Very Young*. Illus. by Ernest H. Shepard. New York: E. P. Dutton, 1961. 102 pp.

Opie, Iona and Peter, eds. *The Oxford Dictionary of Nursery Rhymes*. London: Oxford University, 1951. 467 pp.

8

Easy Access

How can we build the easy access roads that will lead the church on to the strong span, the two-way thoroughfare? What can we do to create the climate where reading is just naturally part of what a congregation does and talks about? How can we develop a reading church, a church where children and adults read the literature of childhood and share it with each other?

Our answer falls into two parts that are intertwined and draw nourishment from each other. One is concrete, the other intangible. Perhaps the intangible is the essential ingredient. It has to do with attitude, enthusiasm, milieu. The excitement of exchanging ideas is contagious. If you can get that going, the rest will take some work, but it will be fun as well as gratifying. The other part consists of programming suggestions that will help create this attitude by underscoring the importance of reading in the Christian life and by connecting people and books.

Developing a Reading Climate

Talk About Books You Have Read

Mention them in sermons, classes, Christian Education meetings, workshops. Share your enthusiasm with friends; share the books themselves; pass them around. Have a reading bulletin board where readers of all ages tack up recommendations and comments. Among people who have never really talked much about books, you will find hesitancy about voicing opinions. Adults may be self-conscious about reading books for the young. These inhibitions soon disappear in an atmosphere of acceptance and interest.

Provide a Library

Set up a budget for new materials and make a space, however limited, for good fiction. (We know a church librarian who once threw out *The Magician's Nephew* and *Crime and Punishment* because the occult and

mysteries had no place in the church.) Running a library is expensive, and most likely you will not be able to rely on your church library exclusively for the kind of reading we are talking about. Nevertheless, the library should be a viable part of the church program, and it should encourage church members of all ages to study, research, and read for pleasure.

Provide Books

If there is no space or money for a full-fledged church library, you can arrange a shelf in the hall, a circulating cart, a box of good summer reading. In one church, members lent or exchanged children's books they had enjoyed; one person sent out cards once a month so that all volumes were returned and eventually found their way home. Even a limited number of books, if made easily available, will contribute to the creation of a reading climate.

Establish a Committee

A church library needs a strong and active committee, part of whose expressed charge is to encourage reading. Even without a library, some team concerned with connecting books and people needs a slot in the organization. Such a team or committee needs to work closely with the church staff so that motivational activities can fit into the total program of the church, and the church needs communication with the committee to inform them of study courses and emphases that can be enriched by books. The committee will plan programs and publicity and will recruit others to help. As both a policy-making group and a working committee, it will require in many ways the involvement of different age groups within the congregation.

Insure Visibility

Make the location of books—whether a separate room or a table top in the hall—a place where people will want to come to browse, to check out materials, or to spend a few minutes reading. Try not to schedule meetings there, to avoid limiting its accessibility. If it cannot be staffed, post clear, visible, easily understood instructions about borrowing books. Have attractive displays, bulletin boards, and book lists. Around the church have signs locating the library and inviting people to come; put up posters mentioning new materials and special programs. Send out a library newsletter at regular intervals. Distribute flyers and book lists in church bulletins. Have an annual book fair and sale.

Share Book Content in Different Settings

One of the best ways to share the content of books is through special programs. By programs we mean occasions where we deliberately talk about the content of children's books in a group setting. As you move towards establishing programs for reading and sharing in your church, you should first consider the many possible settings where such programs would be appropriate.

(1) Intergenerational Church School Hours. Here you might have a ten- or fifteen-minute booktalk, a storytelling session, a film adaptation of a book and discussion afterwards, a readers theater involving readers from a range of ages, or a panel book discussion. Try these suggestions at church school during August, the summer, or perhaps on every fifth Sunday.

(2) Church Night Suppers. Present a puppet show adapted from a book like *Clotilda's Magic* by Kent or *The Quarreling Book* by Zolotow. Try a panel book discussion with adults and youth on the panel.

(3) Committee Meetings. A ten-minute booktalk can be centered around a particular theme or subject at the beginning of the Nurture, Worship, or Education councils. Reading aloud from a pertinent passage can open a Women of the Church or Circle meeting.

(4) Church School Classes. All grades and ages can have regularly scheduled times when members of the library committee give out book lists, talk about new acquisitions, and answer questions.

(5) Book Discussion Groups. These can be organized by grades or by age groups, but make sure the adults read some children's books. Experiment with an intergenerational group, making sure children are comfortable expressing themselves. Discuss the same book in an adult group and a children's group and compare notes.

The principle is this: never lose an opportunity to encourage the use of children's literature. Do this by creating an atmosphere in which the exchange of ideas is enjoyed and appreciated, and connections with the Christian life are recognized and shared. Make books available. Involve people. Publicize, promote, and then program.

Programming for a Reading Church

You are committed to developing a reading church; you see times and places where people can learn about books. Where do you go from here? Many of the following suggestions come from local library programs. Although many were initially planned for children, they can be equally effective for all age groups. Several of these techniques require more instructions than can be given in this summary. In each instance, some book in the adult bibliography will offer what you need in more detail.

Program format need be limited only by your energy, time, and imagination. One of our best programs was a musical of borrowed Broadway show tunes and an original libretto. In this case the musical was to promote the use of the library. Alas, the script is gone. That is probably just as well, for we remember one scene where someone appeared from outer space and said, "Take me to your Reader." The show may not have been great art, but it was certainly great fun. We involved people of all ages and presented it at family night supper after magnificent publicity (flyers designed and delivered by fifth graders). As a result, the congregation started using the library! We can guarantee that good programming will help stimulate interest. You may not be up to writing an "off" Broadway musical; we never were again. Here are some less strenuous, tried and true methods of programming.

Booktalks

Booktalks can be formal or informal. Simply telling someone about a book in conversation or mentioning a book in a sermon or speech is a kind of informal booktalk. What we are recommending here, however, is a more formal talk—a presentation specifically about books, for a particular audience. The books discussed within the talk may be totally unrelated, but the presentation often works well when the books are tied together by a common theme or idea. Several books by the same author—perhaps Eleanor Cameron, Katherine Paterson, or Betsy Byars—make a good program.

A unit of study or a series of lectures can be initiated by a ten-minute booktalk on titles that have relevance to the topic. For example, the two books in the sample booktalk below raise interesting questions about God's plan for individual lives, about the destiny of nations. You could add *Johnny Tremain* by Esther Forbes and *My Brother Sam Is Dead* by the Colliers. These titles explore from different angles the themes of loyalty and patriotism.

Here is a sample, followed by some pointers.

Sample Booktalk:
Julia and the Hand of God by Eleanor Cameron
and *Homesick* by Jean Fritz.

Julia Redfern, her mother and brother live with her grandmother in San Francisco shortly after the First World War. Julia is fascinated by tales of the San Francisco earthquake. Her grandmother says it was the Hand of God destroying an evil city. Julia listens and is intrigued by other strange tales she hears—an uncle killed in France who appeared at the foot of his sister's bed on the night of his death, unexplained sounds like those of a beloved dead pet, a warning trill of notes from a bird. How strange everything is.

And how is it that she can never stay out of scrapes? One day she and her friend Maisie try to cremate a dead mouse in Maisie's mother's best cooking pot. It seems a perfectly harmless activity, not a deliberately wicked or naughty thing to do. But it causes so much trouble: the terrible aroma it makes; the pot, belonging to a family where every penny has to count, that is ruined; and worst of all, the friend who does not assume part of the responsibility and turns the afternoon's play into a disaster with far-reaching consequences.

For one thing, Julia has to earn money to pay for the pot. In the course of doing that, she meets a person she might otherwise not have known, a retired art historian with an invaluable art collection. Then she becomes part of a harrowing adventure when a roaring fire threatens part of San Francisco and Julia has her own encounter with the Hand of God. Julia is a memorable character, as are other members of her family. This book has many facets and makes thought-provoking reading.

Julia is very like Jean Fritz, who wrote a fictionalized account of her childhood in China during the twenties. In her story called *Homesick*, Jean wants more than anything else to return to America where, she believes, everything will be different. She understands what it means to be an alien. She hates singing "God Save the King" in the British school she has to attend and has a painfully unpleasant encounter with the class bully one day when she refuses to sing. She declares she will never attend school again. Her father, after listening to her tale of woe, has an inspiration. He teaches her the words of "My Country 'tis of Thee" which she can sing at the same time to the same tune. In school the next day the bully is satisfied with her participation, not realizing she is singing words that mean so much to her about her own country.

One day when she skips school and goes down by the river, she meets another child who calls her a foreign devil. What happens as a result of this encounter? Does she ever see the boy again? What does one's own country and place to belong mean? This book won the American Book Award in Children's Hardback Fiction in 1982.

Pointers:

(1) The technique of giving a booktalk comes with practice. Memorize the talk, write it out, or use notes—however you are comfortable. In any case, you will have to practice. Spend some time in private rehearsal.

(2) Familiarize yourself with the main events, a funny incident, a favorite character. Know the points you want to make that will stimulate interest.

(3) Do not tell the whole story—just enough to make another person want to experience the book. Never tell the ending.

(4) Have the book on hand, preferably *in* hand, when you are talking about it.

(5) Maintain your credibility. Be careful not to oversell a book or make it better than it really is.

(6) Be prepared to lend the book if possible. You and the recipient will enjoy the satisfaction of an immediate transfer. Pass out the books as you finish talking about them and have a plan for recording names of borrowers. Also have a separate sign-up sheet so that listeners can be assured of a chance to read any book they wish to.

Book Discussions

These are for persons who want to discover added dimensions in a book. They want to hear what someone else thinks. This type of program requires a leader or moderator who will stimulate discussion with questions and help the group focus on the significant themes and issues. A good moderator is able to draw insights from participants, and, if the group is intergenerational, is sensitive to those who may have less verbal skill. Book discussions work best when participation is voluntary. Here are two models.

Panel book discussion. A panel of five persons reads *The Prydain Chronicles,* a series of five books by Lloyd Alexander. (See Ch. 11 for themes and values in these books.) Each member of the panel will have read all five books and will be responsible for one in depth. Each will present a brief statement about one book; then the moderator will open the floor for questions and comments which the whole group may direct to the panel. This is a good way to introduce a book or a series of books that is unknown to the audience.

Round table discussion. All participants have read the book(s) and have equal say. The moderator may begin the discussion with a short critical commentary and will help the group clarify the main themes. Try *A*

Wizard of Earthsea by Le Guin for this. You will need to locate or order extra copies of the book so everyone will have had a chance to read it.

Read-Alouds

A book, an episode from a book, or a chapter is read to listeners. This technique is most effective with preschool, elementary, and intergenerational groups. Often books are read a chapter at a time during each group session. White's *Charlotte's Web* or Caudill's *Did You Carry the Flag Today, Charley?* are naturals for this kind of experience. Yashima's *Crow Boy,* in picture book format, is a powerful story that works well even without the pictures. The *Moffat* books by Estes are episodic, so they can be read from time to time without destroying the story line. Laughlin's *The Little Leftover Witch* is excellent intergenerational fare.

Pointers:

(1) Any reader should read the story aloud ahead of time to get used to the rhythm and cadence of the words, to be sure of pronunciation, and to listen with critical ear to the sound of his or her voice.

(2) Allow time for questions or comments afterwards, but do not force this.

(3) Reading picture books with younger children requires special preparation. Pictures need to be shown at the same time the text is heard. To do this you must be familiar enough with the story to read it upside down, sideways, and sometimes with your eyes shut, because you must hold the book before the group in such a way that all the children can see the pictures. The combination of picture and word underscores for the very young child the meaning inherent in the story. Good picture books for group presentation have large, clear pictures that can be comprehended easily from a short distance.

Read-Alouds Using Children and Youth

Another effective way to use reading aloud is to let older children read to younger children. This is a method in which both listener and reader gain, and it proves again that teaching is one of the best learning experiences. Choose from this list: *Alexander and the Terrible, Horrible, No Good, Very Bad Day* by Viorst, *Black Is Brown Is Tan* by Adoff, *Frederick* by Lionni, *Goodnight Moon* and *The Runaway Bunny* by Brown, *Play with Me* by Ets, and *The Carrot Seed* by Krauss.

Pointers:

(1) This activity requires planning with the staff, the education committee, and others so that you have an idea about when this service will be needed. Moving children from one group to another requires coordination.

(2) Enlist readers. Talk about reasons for this kind of sharing, occasions when they will read, what they will need to give in time and preparation. Reading aloud could be a service project for a church school class or a junior high group.

(3) Prepare the readers. Inform and enlist parents' help. Let the children read to each other and evaluate what they do.

(4) Let the readers have choice about what they wish to read. Provide a wide selection from which to choose. Time spent in selection is educational and enjoyable.

Storytelling

One teller and one listener, or one teller and a group of listeners, caught in the spell of a story told without props or book has an immediacy that no other form of communication has except conversation, which is, after all, a kind of storytelling. Storytelling requires skill, and many books can be of help. The important point is that anyone who wants to can tell stories. Be aware, however, that not all stories are meant for the listening experience. Some of the story collections at the end of Ch. 7 are good sources.

Bible stories were first heard rather than read. The lives of Jacob, Joseph, Moses, and David need to be recreated as stories, not study. We may then place them in context, talk about themes, and connect them with other stories. . . . *And Now Miguel* by Krumgold and *The Loner* by Wier are stories of shepherds and shepherd life that can extend the story of David. *The Bronze Bow* by Speare will add rich detail to New Testament stories.

One of our favorite stories for telling to young children is Minarik's *A Kiss for Little Bear.* Although the pictures are charming and should not be missed, they are not for group sharing because of their size. The story, a gentle, warm, and humorous tale, can be told alone. Little Bear sends his grandmother a picture, and she, in turn, sends him a kiss by way of Hen, Frog, Cat, and Skunk. Not only is the kiss delivered, but there is an added dividend and love is multiplied.

Storytelling Using Props

Using props simply means embellishing your storytelling with some sort of visual or aural aid—flannel boards, story hats, story aprons, finger puppets, and so on. (See Bauer's *This Way to Books.*)

A recent workshop in Florida presented Kent's *There's No Such Thing as a Dragon,* a book that quickly and humorously echoes Le Guin's more serious treatment of the theme. These inexpensive props enhanced the story:

(1) A house drawn on poster board. One side showed the interior of the house divided into four

rooms, two upstairs and two downstairs. Windows were cut out and both sides were covered with clear plastic.

(2) A sheet of blue poster board (28″ × 36″) as the first background.

(3) A poster board with only dragon scales painted on it; a head and tail were fastened to this with brads.

(4) Figures for Billy, his mother, his father, and the dragon in several sizes.

(5) An easel.

The story began with the interior of the house propped on the easel with blue poster board background. As the dragon grew, larger figures replaced previous ones. Finally when the dragon picked up the house on his back and walked away, the house was reversed to show the exterior, and the blue poster board was replaced by one covered with dragon scales with head and tail attached.

The props made it possible to include the visual aspects of this story; the fun of seeing the dragon grow along with the sternly repeated words of the mother—"Billy, there's no such thing as a dragon"—was a delightful addition.

Pointers:

(1) Each story is different. Props can be distracting gimmicks rather than helps. Use good judgment.

(2) Props take time and effort. Save them, share them, store them, and catalogue them so they can be found again.

(3) The storyteller does not have to make all the props. This is a good way to involve others.

Readers Theater

This requires writing a kind of script from the actual text of a work, dividing it into parts, and then presenting the story or a portion of it to others. It demands careful analysis of the text, selecting sections to be read, and insuring that those who read have a certain amount of natural "ham" and good voice projection. In some instances churches have a continuing readers theater group or class that studies, prepares, and presents selected books or book portions.

Chapter 8 in Cleary's *Ramona Quimby, Age 8* lends itself to this kind of presentation. Thurber's *The Wonderful O* and *The Thirteen Clocks* make good intergenerational reading. Selected conversations from *Henry 3* by Krumgold are also effective.

Creative Dramatics

For many reasons—most to be lamented—drama almost always works well with children, seldom with adults. It requires telling or reading the story or basic plot outline, letting children discuss, then "playing like" the story really happened to them. Characters use their own dialogue and are encouraged to extrapolate and

embellish within the framework of the story. Much emphasis is placed on portraying the feelings of the characters so that children will come to understand and have empathy for people or animals in circumstances other than their own. New insights often arise from this form of using literature. Try Zolotow's *The Hating Book* with young children, with plenty of time afterward to talk about how we handle our "bad" feelings. Paulin's *Creative Use of Children's Literature* is most helpful here.

Adaptations of Books and Stories

We are speaking here of comic books, films, cassettes, records, and plays. Let us distinguish between two kinds of adaptation.

A third-grade class read several books, selected Hoban's *A Baby Sister for Frances* as a good book for the kindergarten class, wrote a script, made puppets, and presented the story to the children in the kindergarten. In the process they had to get the facts, decide what was important, rephrase ideas, and express them in visual action. Throughout this planning, they had to be aware of the kindergarten as audience. This was a very demanding and creative learning process. The kindergarten children, who already knew the story, loved recalling it this way, affirmed the third graders by their response, and then went back to the book with renewed enthusiasm. That is the best kind of adaptation.

When adaptations are made by adults, particularly for children, we need to ask some questions. What is left out? What has been added? Has the format deprived the audience of the opportunity to imagine? Will it produce a kind of uniform vision or understanding? Any adaptation needs to be evaluated by the original and by the receiver's possible perception.

A Special Word About Audio-Visuals

There are, of course, other ways of communicating, sharing information, and telling stories. More and more often, we find ourselves in a civilization where one does not have to read, though we suspect we will always have symbols to decode and experience to be encoded in some sort of visual, oral, or aural form.

Currently children's literature means what is written down for children to read or hear or for adults to read or tell to them. But even now, that material is leaving print form and being translated into other formats. Often the translation is a transformation; a work can become entirely different on TV or film or audiocassette. Sometimes the new form is as true as it can be to the original, but always it is changed. The brain's process in translating the printed word is not the same as transmitting an image or sound, and we are not even sure whether the final outcome is the same. Each new format requires a new evaluation.

How do we judge a story in a different medium? One way is by its faithfulness to the original, but that may not be the only criterion or the one that demands the most integrity. Instead, try to maintain the independence to look at each separate piece as if it were a new work of art, judging it by what it accomplishes in its new medium.

When a writer sells rights for a work to become a film, record, or TV program, he or she should realize that what follows will be an offspring, not a clone. It must be judged, as our own offspring ultimately are, by its individual and peculiar merits. So do not accept or reject another format because you have either loved or hated the book by the same name. Preview it carefully in its own right before you use it. Even so, there's no question that book sales zoom every time a title is translated into a new AV medium.

Filmstrips make picture books available for a larger group. Weston Woods Studios in Connecticut does animations and iconographs of children's picture books. *Rosie's Walk* by Hutchins, for example, is a charming book; the film is a masterful combination of picture and music. If you want to use Marcia Brown's *Stone Soup* at a church night supper, it will have to be as a filmstrip. The book could be seen only by a smaller group.

Armstrong's *Sounder* is in its own right a fine film, but it is quite different from the book, which is a profound literary experience and should not be missed. Barbara Robinson's *The Best Christmas Pageant Ever,* Paterson's *The Great Gilly Hopkins,* the books of Dr. Seuss, and *Cinderella* have all been translated into television specials. The two points to remember are: judge each work apart from the book, and have the book on hand for checkout after the presentation.

Where can you find out which books have been adapted to some audio-visual format? Our bibliography occasionally gives this information, and also suggests an inexpensive paperback multimedia guide. A number of books include this kind of information. Paulin's *Creative Uses of Children's Literature,* for example, lists *Little Women* both as a film and as two different sets of records.

Where will you get these audio-visuals? Some may be checked out of a public library; some are carried by local bookstores. When all else fails, *Children's Media Marketplace* is a directory of sources for locating children's materials. It gives names and addresses of publishers and distributors, and lists different kinds of materials arranged by name, subject, and format. It is designed to answer such questions as: Where can I find materials for handicapped children? Who distributes films made by children? Who distributes media in Spanish and Portuguese?

Creating easy access is something you can do with just a little thought if you remember these three approaches: (1) motivate people to read, through casual and intentional sharing; (2) make plans that include books as part of most of the church's activities; (3) offer varied programs in many settings. The destination is a two-way span that makes intergenerational communication and community an exciting likelihood.

9

Toll Free

How can we use the stories of childhood in communicating the Christian faith?

Our answer to this question is what we call a bonus or fringe benefit of good reading. Ideas for using books and stories evolve from literature's largesse. So this is the conclusion, not the beginning of the conversation. If you have begun the process of reading and listening to children's literature, you are already making connections, learning techniques of communication. Nevertheless, here are some suggestions about *how*—how to use books to build community, how to preach inclusively, and how to educate in planned situations. You can find all of the books we mention in the bibliographies.

Toll Free Bridges into Community

Christian community is a gift. We cannot grit our teeth and achieve it, but we can nurture and express it. Developing individual relationships; supporting the basic units of our community, the homes; offering help and concern when troubles come; serving, playing, and worshiping together—these are the ways we build community. Good books for children have something to offer in all of these situations.

Use Children's Books as Gifts

Choose hardbacks for permanency and beauty, paperbacks for convenience and economy. Most of the books we have mentioned are published in paperback, so price is a point in their favor. We like to celebrate birthdays, new babies, arrivals and departures, new homes, graduations, and special achievements, not to mention holidays and Holy Days, with appropriate books. A thoughtfully chosen book is a sure sign of interest and love, for both children and adults.

Hearne's *Choosing Books for Children* is a promising welcome for a new baby, while *The Very Little Boy* by Krasilovsky or Hoban's *A Baby Sister for Frances*

helps and entertains older siblings. "With thanks for a home that welcomes all ages" said a card accompanying *Noah's Ark* by Spier, a housewarming gift. A busy, pressured executive received as a birthday card Viorst's *Alexander and the Terrible, Horrible,* etc. along with a new perspective on problems. As you become acquainted with the books in our bibliographies and with books you discover yourself, you will find that the matching of people, occasions, and books comes easily.

Use Children's Literature to Build Relationships

Sharing a good book is a way of giving yourself. If you find it difficult to talk with children and would like to express an interest, you can create some strong bonds with an hour or two of reading together. We know a parish shepherd who offers an hour of read-aloud time for the children of each family in her flock. She arranges a date at her house or theirs or in the park. If you choose this way to make friends with young children, remember that the younger the child, the more books you need to have on hand. Be prepared to read some books four times, and do not take it personally if children reject a book in the middle of the story. A great thing about reading to children is that you cannot be a bore; they will not let you.

Some of our best friends are middle schoolers and high school students who have discovered the books of George MacDonald or Madeleine L'Engle through our recommendations; who have found new approaches to American history through *Johnny Tremain* by Forbes or the Colliers' *My Brother Sam Is Dead;* who have encountered key ideas for a civics class in Christopher's *The White Mountains.*

You are offering the book as an interested friend, not as an English teacher. There are no penalties if the book is not read, no requirements for a report, and no personal rejection if tastes and needs differ. With this kind of pressure-free interest, young people are able to respond as they choose. A comfortable climate develops in which opinions are shared despite age differences, and the reasons for a reaction are deemed as important as the reaction itself.

Perhaps a more important way to establish relationships with young people is to read the books that they are required to read in school or that they recommend to you. Most high school students, for example, are required to read *Huckleberry Finn*. If you have read it too, you have some knowledge of what they are learning and some possible reference points for conversation and teaching.

Use Children's Books
to Support Families

Good books help us minister to families. Information about books will strengthen two foundations of family life: shared pleasure and communication. Parents who want to say something about their faith but lack words will find a starting place in MacDonald's fantasies or Lewis' Narnia Chronicles when they read them with their children. *Bridge to Terabithia* by Paterson or *The Magic Moth* by Lee can be a catalyst for sharing fears and hopes about death. Cleary, Estes, and L'Engle present positive pictures of real families that struggle with problems.

The church that highlights books for seasonal reading, books that enrich units of Bible study, books that are fun for family vacations, or a basic list of books for toddlers, is giving useful, life-shaping information to parents who may be too busy or unsure to gain such information on their own. We know of a church that solicits family book reviews and publishes them twice a year in the newsletter, along with a prayer for good readers and good reading.

One church, in a community without a local bookstore, held a book fair each year. Plans were made in cooperation with the closest denominational bookstore, which sent requested books and some additional titles on consignment. The fall date encouraged the giving of books for Christmas. In conjunction with the fair there was an intergenerational session on good books to read. Afterward there was a session on reading with children, for parents and teachers only.

Books for and about children will prove to be rich resources as we try to help parents communicate with their children. A parent support group could read and discuss Krumgold's *Henry 3*, Waldron's *The Integration of Mary-Larkin Thornhill*, and Krumgold's *Onion John*. Each of these books presents a situation in which the parents want something for their children and ask something of their children. Discussing these fictional situations allows for some distance and enables parents

to be more objective. It allows them to make connections that they can use when dealing with their offspring in real life. Parents need to read books that explore the pain and destruction of relationships, as well as those that emphasize the growth and hope flourishing in loving families.

Use Children's Literature
for Pastoral Care

Pastors are not the only source of pastoral care in the church. They cannot possibly be. The rest of us, whether called pastors are not, are responsible for caring about whatever helps or hurts the other members of our community. The following suggestions are made for everyone who cares about others.

The right book can shed light on a student's fear, give a teacher insight into an emotional problem, or help a child who is facing a stressful situation. Parents of a handicapped baby, for example, found *Father's Arcane Daughter* by Konigsberg to be a source of encouragement. Young people struggling with family relationships find support and understanding from stories like Paterson's *Jacob Have I Loved* and L'Engle's *Meet the Austins*. *Shadow of a Bull* by Wojciechowska leads young people through the experience of facing adult expectations at odds with their own dreams. *Henry 3* was valuable to a parent who dreaded the growing independence of her teenage son. A list of a dozen good preschool books helped relieve the anxiety of a grandmother who was assuming care of a young child.

In the adult bibliography are several books grouping titles by subjects that concern children and youth. They are good places to look if you have a definite situation in mind such as death, divorce, intense school competition, vocational decisions, or fears. One important word of caution, however, is never to recommend a book which you have not read and appreciated yourself. You are offering not simply information, but sensitive understanding and a responsible form of pastoral care.

Use Children's Books
for Service

When the young people at church led recreation each week at a housing development, some of them found that a quiet corner for a read-aloud session was always popular. Wisely, they chose several books and read in small enough groups to maintain a feeling of individual attention. The church library committee worked with the youth in selecting a variety of titles.

One church we know selected reading matter for inmates in the city jail. Juvenile fiction titles were the staples of this program, which had been requested by the jail officials. Another church, frequently visited by transients, kept a box of good discarded books to give to children in the families. Appropriate secondhand books in good condition can be an excellent resource for serving many persons. Apart from whatever good accrues to those served, we find that a strong sense of community develops in the group that extends its circle of care beyond its own boundaries.

Use Children's Literature for Recreation

Playing together is an important part of community, and books should have a part in our recreation together. A Christmas party for the first and second grades ended with reading Wenning's *The Christmas Mouse* and then singing "Silent Night." During rest hour and at bedtime, a camp counselor read Alexander's *The Book of Three* to his cabin. At a church family picnic a storyteller enthralled the campfire group with some of the *Jack Tales*. Another church's once-a-week recreation day during the summer includes a story hour.

Behind all of these fruitful uses of reading in the church community lies a knowledge of children's literature. Which books will be valuable for which group? Which will fit the time schedule? Which will measure up to the highest literary standards possible? Only readers can answer these questions. Happy is the church that has several persons who know the books children love.

Use Children's Literature in Inclusive Preaching

We have spoken of children's stories as an intergenerational language in situations where the spoken word may be a barrier. Using books and stories that children know is an inclusive act, a demonstration of the faith that all members of the Body of Christ are valuable and responsible. A subtle but very real change takes place when children listen to a minister who knows what has been exciting and interesting to them. Fortunately, these stories speak as clearly to adults as to children.

The congregation already shares a literary vocabulary. The nonsense of Mother Goose gives us a cast of quickly sketched, memorable characters: Jack Sprat and his wife, different and complementary; Little Jack Horner, so proud of an action not notably praiseworthy; Little Boy Blue, asleep on the job. Set the role of biblical scholar aside for a moment and take an anthology of these rhymes. Some are sheer sound and whimsy; others sing of people, emotions, events that we recognize. Try condensing the theme of each rhyme to one word.

Fairy tales grow from stories and situations that are ageless concerns: sibling rivalry, impossible challenges and quests, suffering through evil and our own human folly, high hopes and the triumph of right. Cinderella, the Fisherman's Wife, Beauty and the Beast, Pinnochio, and the Ugly Duckling belong to adults and children alike.

A book or story can set the stage or introduce a sermon's theme. For example, a sermon on the meaning of repentance might begin this way:

One of our first tasks in life is to match sounds and meanings. The sound "no" is a good example, as anyone who has lived with a two-year-old can testify. Beginning in third grade we learn to use a book that helps us find word meanings, a dictionary. We must understand what the word represents if we are to communicate, follow instructions, or learn new facts. It is difficult not to know a word's meaning; it is worse to think we know it, and act as if we know it when we do not know what the word means at all.

Children, and those of us who read to children, have probably met Peggy Parish's character, Amelia Bedelia. She is a housemaid who always thinks she knows what the instructions mean. She starts the day's work with a list of tasks in her hand; "Change the towels in the green bathroom" comes first. She is puzzled. Why change such nice towels? But she gets some scissors and snips here and there until the towels are changed. To Amelia Bedelia, "Dust the furniture" means sprinkle dusting powder all over the living room, and "drawing the drapes when the sun comes in" stands for sitting down with paper and pencil to draw the drapes. "Dress the chicken" is the last bit of work, and you have probably already guessed how Amelia Bedelia does that. "I wonder if she wants a he chicken or a she chicken?" said Amelia Bedelia as she assembled needle, thread, and cloth.

I am afraid that many of us are like Amelia Bedelia when we hear in our scripture today the words of Jesus: "The time is fulfilled, and the kingdom of God is at hand; repent, and believe in the gospel" (Mark 1:15). We think we know what "repent" means—be sorry, feel bad, not do what is wrong anymore. By acting on this misunderstanding, we miss what it is Jesus is calling on us to do.

A common theme of fairy tales opens the door for "The Key to Getting What We Want," a sermon on prayer:

Once upon a time a young soldier was returning from the war. He met an old woman in the woods who said, "If you'll climb down to the room beneath the roots of this old tree and bring back the box in the third room, I will pay you. But the soldier discovered that rubbing the box summoned a large dog that would grant anything he wanted. And that, of course, was much better than the old woman's promise of money.

Another story tells us that in order to win the princess of his dreams and the kingdom as well, the youngest son sails to the end of the world, slays the dragon, and finds the gold key that unlocks the door to riches and power and love. The story always ends, "And they lived happily ever after." The hero and, we hope, the heroine got all that they wished for.

These stories are about us, really, for we have an unlimited supply of wishes, wishes that seem to be out of reach. I wish I had health, I wish I could pass math without studying, I wish I could go to Disney World whenever I like, I wish nobody in the world was hungry or cold, I wish I could discover the cure for cancer. If only we had the magic box or the golden key. . . . It is something we have all thought and felt, and so it makes our scripture seem to be a particularly welcome word: "Whatever you ask in my name, I will do it." And it makes it particularly important that we hear the whole word.

Because these writers are skilled in saying much with few words, you will find their works filled with memorable passages. Lena, in Sebestyen's *Words by Heart*, struggles to honor her father's request that she save the boy, Tater Haney, who has mortally wounded him. As she looks down at Tater, she asks silently, "Papa, why couldn't you give up on him?" Then she moves to honor her father's request: "She couldn't love him. But she loved someone who knew how to love him, and that was a beginning" (148–9). It would be hard to find a better summary of the way to peace in personal or international relations.

In Hoban's *A Bargain for Frances* Thelma tricks Frances and Frances gets even. When Thelma observes that she will have to be careful in future dealings, Frances asks, "Do you want to be careful, or do you want to be friends?" (55). Relationships are risky.

Princess Irene begs her grandmother to be visible to Curdie so he will believe she exists, and the grandmother answers, "Seeing is not believing—it is only seeing" (MacDonald 1979, 418). Thurber's Duke of Coffin Castle *(The Thirteen Clocks)* says, "We all have flaws, and mine is being wicked" (114).

Read first, keep a card file with page numbers, and soon connections will develop. If a phrase or situation speaks to you and makes an idea clear or lively, then it will probably do the same for others, and in this case, the others will include the youngest listeners.

10

Bridge Designs

Children's literature has a place in the church's planned education. Like all resources, it must be judged. Does it contribute to the goals and objectives of this study? Does it fit the needs and abilities of these students? Is it practical and available for this situation? We think the answer will often, though not always, be "yes." Here are some designs that you could adapt and improve for local bridges into learning.

A Workshop for Kindergarten Leaders

We have suggested that children's books are an excellent way for adults to learn about children. Picture books are brief, clear, simple tools for teacher training. They can help parents and teachers get an overview of child development. The following is an outline for a two-hour leadership event for kindergarten teachers of diverse background and experience. The format could be modified and the books changed for leaders of other age groups.

The purpose of this workshop is to increase our knowledge and understanding of kindergarten children through recalling our own childhood, through looking at books that show us children, through connecting new understanding with our teaching, and through praying for our pupils. The session will be most valuable if teachers have the curriculum they will be teaching and their class roll. If the curriculum supplies an overview of child development, include this as a resource.

Workshop Outline

(1) Remembering. Those who communicate well with children stay in touch with their own childhood.

Materials needed: Pictures of kindergarten children engaged in typical activities to stimulate memories; sand timers, one for every two or three persons.

Instructions (printed or verbal): Recall a childhood experience during the two years before first grade. Try to remember the event, the persons involved, your feelings, and as many sensory details as possible. Find a partner and share this memory. Use the sand timer, three minutes apiece for each of you. This is good practice for the kindergarten attention span.

Summarize with these questions: Was remembering difficult? What stands out the most—feelings, events, setting, people? Which feelings and experiences do you think your pupils will have shared?

(2) Looking at books.

Materials needed: Books and printed study guide for each participant.

Anderson, *The Wonderful Shrinking Shirt;* Bridwell, *Clifford the Small Red Puppy;* Brown, *The Dead Bird, The Runaway Bunny;* Burningham, *Mr. Gumpy's Outing;* Burton, *The Little House;* Ets, *Play with Me;* Gág, *Millions of Cats;* Gauch, *Christina Katerina and the Box;* Heide, *The Shrinking of Treehorn;* Hoban, *A Baby Sister for Frances, (Bedtime for Frances, A Birthday for Frances);* Hutchins, *Titch;* Kellogg, *The Mystery of the Missing Red Mitten;* Krasilovsky, *The Very Little Boy;* Kraus, *Leo the Late Bloomer;* Kuskin, *Just Like Everyone Else;* Lionni, *Swimmy;* Minarik, *A Kiss for Little Bear;* Ness, *Sam, Bangs & Moonshine;* Sendak, *The Nutshell Library* and *Where the Wild Things Are;* Silverstein, *Where the Sidewalk Ends;* Udry, *Let's Be Enemies;* Viorst, *Alexander and the Terrible, Horrible, No Good, Very Bad Day;* Waber, *Ira Sleeps Over;* Zolotow, *The Hating Book.*

By checking themes and values in the bibliography you will get some idea of what each of these books tells us about the kindergarten child. You can probably add to the list or substitute when these titles are not available. Hutchins' *Titch* and Krasilovsky's *The Very Little Boy,* for example, show children's concern with size, their lack of power, their interest in stories about children like themselves. These books illustrate the necessity for simple plot, limited number of characters, single theme, and clear, uncluttered visual presentation. Either of these books will do, and there are many others that convey the same ideas.

Instructions: With a partner choose a book; read it out loud; look at it with the study guide; from your observations, record one or two statements about kindergarten children. Choose another book and repeat the process. Be prepared to share with the whole group the following: five adjectives describing the kindergartener, one need, one ability, one interest, and one problem.

Allow time for group sharing, either accepting verbal responses or getting participants to write observations on newsprint as they complete a book.

Study Guide: After reading the book, look again and note:

The book—its appearance, size, layout, style of pictures, blank space.

The story—the subject, sequence of events, number of people, feelings expressed.

The style—length, vocabulary, sentence length, repetition, rhythm.

The child—interests, abilities, relationships, feelings, needs, problems. These may be displayed in a story with a child as a character or inferred from the subject and the way it is presented.

(3) Connecting these ideas with teaching. If teaching teams are present, they should work together. If they have received and studied the list of pupils in advance, the planning can be more detailed.

Materials needed: Curriculum and printed instructions.

Instructions: With some of the things we have observed about kindergarten children in mind, talk about and record:

One change you will make in your room arrangement.

One thing you will do to make the room visually appealing.

Any changes to make the session theme fit the needs and interests of kindergarten children.

How the theme or main ideas can be communicated best.

(4) Praying for students.

Materials needed: class rolls. A few songs kindergarten children like to sing. A leader prepared to tell the story of Jesus and the children in a way that demonstrates good storytelling.

Draw the study to a close with songs, the story, and a time of prayer.

Instructions: The leader needs to make a few closing remarks, such as the following: Every child we teach is individual, is unique, fits no pattern, and has his or her own gifts and needs. Thoughtful prayer helps us understand our children as nothing else can. Use your class roll now in silence to name your children.

A Stewardship Study for the Congregation

A filmstrip of Marcia Brown's *Stone Soup* (from Weston Woods) was the basis for a stewardship study that preceded making commitments of time and talents. A church night supper was planned; each household unit was asked to bring an ingredient for stew, fruit or vegetable salad, biscuits, or ice cream. The food was prepared in large cooking pots and the tables set up. When families and individuals finished their part in the cooking, they were asked to look at the wall display.

Around the wall in the fellowship hall were cooking pots drawn on poster board, labeled with service opportunities in the life of the church and the "ingredients" for each opportunity, i.e., Worship: music, vocal or instrumental; liturgist; sanctuary arrangement; planning bulletins; etc. Outreach: United Service Center; Meals on Wheels; planning mission education; etc.

After supper the filmstrip was shown. In small groups these questions were discussed: Why were people unwilling to share what they had? How did the soldiers get them to share? What were the results? What would have happened if some of the people had refused to add what they had?

The small group leader continues: "The life and work of the church are something like *Stone Soup* and our supper tonight. Each of us has something to add, a gift that God has given us for the good of all of us." After reading 1 Corinthians 12:4-11, group members were encouraged to mention gifts they recognized in others in the group. The leader recorded these for use in the closing worship.

Music brought the whole group together. After singing, the scripture was read again. At 1 Corinthians 12:8 ("And to another the Spirit gives the ability to _____"), each group leader continued the naming of gifts on the basis of the group list. The phrase from Corinthians was repeated before each small group leader began.

Everyone left with a list of service opportunities for the coming year, a list bearing the pot from *Stone Soup* as the logo. The logo was repeated on information about stewardship throughout the season.

Uses in Graded Education

When we mention books for church school and other settings of planned learning, especially those planned for children, many persons think of Bible story books. Our bibliography contains a limited number of these, chosen for some particular literary or artistic viewpoint. We include none of the reference books we think are essential for elementary school classes—the Bible dictionaries, atlases, and Bible background resources so important for research and discovery. Instead, we are focusing on the kind of book the church is more likely to overlook: fiction. The Church and Synagogue Library Association provides a well annotated, inexpensive bibliography of religious books for children. Every church should have one on hand.

Let us emphasize once more that any time you want accurate, attractively presented, concise information on any subject—Egyptian pyramids, celebrating Easter in Russia, cathedrals, how to make musical instruments—children's literature is the place to look. Sutherland's *Children and Books* and Larrick's *Parent's Guide* contain very good guides to nonfiction. But we have not attempted to cover this field.

We have included only a few Bible story books. Although we think these should play an important part in classes prior to first grade, we see these as a second step, feeling that stories from the Bible should be *told* first. Before using a Bible story book, talk about the story's connection with the Bible. Mark its location with a bookmark. As children begin to read, their attention should be focused on the Bible itself in some of the good and readable modern translations. In selecting Bible story books be conscious of art work, for it has more impact than words. Have varied styles of art so children will not associate Jesus or David with one single picture. Be cautious about books with imaginary characters. Read the text, checking against biblical text and for the historical validity of imaginary details.

With these thoughts as a preface, let us turn to the use of children's literature in planned education programs such as church school, vacation church school, and youth meetings.

The Preschool Book Table

Here, understanding "why" we use various picture and story books is as important as book suggestions. Most curricula for children before first grade suggest supplementary books for each unit, and a book table or reading corner is part of the room arrangement. If, however, the books are not Bible stories, teachers may feel that these reading suggestions are extraneous material to be ignored or used only as a "break" from real learning.

Education about how children learn and develop prior to age six will help leaders see the value of "secular" books in the classroom. Leaders need to realize that familiar books create a welcoming climate;

reading to one or two children establishes rapport; "secular" and "religious" are not divisions recognized by children—an attitude to be preserved. Furthermore, stories help children's cognitive development (sequencing, comparing verbal and visual media, acquiring vocabulary, testing reality); they provide situations and stimulate recall of situations where God is present in the lives of children; and they extend the world that God loves, helping children appreciate the infinite variety in culture, dress, talents, and persons. The list could go on.

The *Frances* books by Hoban help children to recognize themselves. Udry's *Let's Be Enemies* shows them how to accept and handle their emotions, and through *The Carrot Seed* by Krauss they come to know God's dependable world. *Changes, Changes* by Hutchins is a stimulus to creative action in the block corner, while *Swimmy* by Lionni may do the same thing at the art table. Gauch's *Christina Katerina and the Box* opens up the similar possibilities with a refrigerator carton.

A valuable teacher-training event or classroom demonstration can help leaders know how to use such books well. It could help them know when to simply read the book without comment; how to help children "read" pictures; how to ask questions that require an answer beyond "yes" or "no"; how to control our own "expository demon" (a C. S. Lewis phrase). A picture book from the bibliography could be used in the demonstration. You could compare three Christmas books by Bruna, Kurelek, and Winthrop to get a feel for varied art styles.

Learning About Giving in the First Grade

During Advent, early elementary children were learning about giving—how God has given to us and how we may give to others. In their thinking, tangible things like toys and food and trips were the significant gifts. The leaders had on hand four books that told about gifts, three gifts that were intangible, one that was sacrificial. About ten minutes were spent with each of these books, beginning with an introduction: "This is a story about giving a gift. Listen for what the gift is. Think about what it costs. Is it expensive? Is it a gift you could give? In what ways is it like God's gift to us?"

The books were: Coutant, *The Gift* (slightly condensed); Ness, *Josefina February;* Peterson, *Erik and the Christmas Horse;* Rabe, *The Balancing Girl*. All four books were available for checkout when the unit ended. The books were listed on an information sheet for parents with a statement about their purpose and suggestions for some ways to give "intangibles" during the season.

Studying Earth Stewardship
in the Middle Grades

The study was responsible stewardship of the earth, and one center asked children to think up ways to use things twice. There were several objects that could be recycled. Anderson's *The Wonderful Shrinking Shirt* was a book on the table at this center.

Another center depicted how we treat the earth God has given us. Silverstein's *Where the Sidewalk Ends* was opened to the poem about "Sarah Cynthia Sylvia Stout" as an example of one of our excesses.

At a listening center, verses from Genesis 1 and pictures of people, natural beauty, and animals were posted on the bulletin board. Preparation for listening said: "How do you feel about the world God has made and given us to care for? Listen to some of these voices and add your own." Psalm 8 and verses from Psalm 104 were interspersed with a selection from *The House of Wings* by Byars. A few words sketched the situation, and then the leader read pages 45–47 where the grandfather tells his story. The leader concluded with a portion of Ch. 3 from *Little House on the Prairie* where the father, who must hunt for the family's food, lets the deer go. Paper, pencil, and paint were on hand so pupils could respond.

Thinking Creatively
in the Upper Elementary Class

After studying Genesis 1, fifth- and sixth-grade students looked at creation in three other ways: listening to "The Creation" from *God's Trombones* by James Weldon Johnson, looking at *The Seven Days of Creation* by Fisher, and reading the story of Aslan's creating Narnia through song in Lewis' *The Magician's Nephew*. Pupils had the opportunity to reflect their feelings with clay, music, or writing.

Peacemaking with Picture Books
in a Youth Group

Do not overlook using picture books with youth. Junior and senior highs are usually far enough from these books in time so that they do not feel insulted by the books, but enjoy looking back.

One study was based on passages from the Sermon on the Mount and divided into three programs on peace between persons, peace in the community, and peace among nations. As an introduction to the study, small groups looked at these picture books to identify some of the causes and cures of small-scale wars. The books used were Hoban's *A Bargain for Frances*, de Paola's *The Knight and the Dragon*, Hamada's *The Tears of the Dragon*, Kent's *There's No Such Thing as a Dragon*, Sendak's *Pierre* from *The Nutshell Library* and *Where*

the *Wild Things Are*, Udry's *Let's Be Enemies*, and Zolotow's *The Quarreling Book*.

The conclusion of the study was *Words By Heart*, a novel by Ouida Sebestyen that demonstrates obedience to Jesus' command to love your enemies. Two readers prepared the book, and it was used in several situations in the church. The story was summarized and the last four chapters were read.

Exploring Peer Relationships
Through Fiction with
the Junior Highs

Illustrations from juvenile fiction can furnish the material for discussion when young people may be self-conscious about analyzing personal experiences. *The Hundred Dresses* by Estes, a brief book, shows in its first few chapters how contagious cruelty can be. In Burch's *Ida Early Comes over the Mountain*, the Sutton children are silent because of peer pressure when their friend, Ida, is ridiculed (81–87), and an excellent example of how to say "I'm sorry" follows on pages 110–117. *How to Eat Fried Worms* by Rockwell is a funny example of how a simple conversation can escalate into a challenge. The first two or three pages capture the incident. In Burch's *Queenie Peavy* the third chapter, "The Sweet Potato," shows the positive strength that comes from peer support.

Here is a sample of how material from a book may be isolated for a reading center. Let us use *Ida Early* as an example, beginning on page 81, where we want the students to read. It is a paperback book, five by seven inches in size. Use a five-by-seven index card for the following introduction:

"Ida Early is the Sutton children's housekeeper and companion. Since their mother's death she has cared for the children. Her dress, manners, appearance, and housekeeping methods are unusual, but the Sutton family has been too happy since she came to their home to think much of this. Until . . ."

Place the card facing page 81. It is held in place by a clip and serves as a marker as well as an introduction. At the conclusion of the section to be read is another card with questions for thought: What made Ellen keep silent when she could have defended Ida? Did she really do wrong by not speaking up? Should friends always stand up for you? Has anything like this ever happened to you—either as Ida or as Ellen?

If you plan to share material in a group, it is a good idea to give out the sections to be read with this same kind of introduction to the section. This is a simple way to involve students and introduce them to the subject before class. They may want to tell the event in their own words. There is a good chance they will read the entire book.

By cutting from the middle of a file folder a thin rectangle that fits the book's height, you can insert the needed pages through the opening. The folder and the book under the folder can be opened on the table with only the pages to be read showing. The introduction is printed on one page of the folder.

Use Children's Literature to Develop Curriculum

Biblical themes and literary themes overlap, as we have said. In *This Way to Books,* Caroline Bauer suggests a book program built around the theme of "What's in a Name?" (2, 3). Her plans list books and related crafts and activities. Names are important to children, important in the Christian community, and important throughout the Bible. We think of Isaac's name meaning laughter, of Jacob's name being changed, of Moses asking God's name, of the names given Jesus, of Simon becoming Peter. We also have the use of names in baptism when each of us is named. In addition to the books that Bauer suggests, Laughlin's *The Little Leftover Witch,* Wier's *The Loner,* and chapters in the *Princess* books by MacDonald add a theological perspective to the name theme. By combining our knowledge of the Bible with an expert's knowledge of children's literature, we have a study unit in hand. This is only one of many examples.

In the bibliography you will find themes and suggestions that may stimulate your thinking. These only suggest; they neither limit nor exhaust the possibilities. If you have not done so already, turn to the books and let them speak for themselves.

PART IV
Bridge-building Materials

"There's no thief like a bad book" runs an old Italian proverb. We think this bibliography is burglar-proof—that is, none of these books will take your valuable time and energy without offering something in return. We have chosen these books for one or more of the following reasons:

(1) We like them. One or both of us found pleasure and/or understanding in reading and sharing each book on this list. Considering the wide area of choice and the two strong personalities involved, the agreement is remarkable.

(2) Critics like them. Included are some works that knowledgeable judges consider the best. We have listed the book awards and their guidelines so you can tell why a book has been singled out. A book receiving the Newbery, Carnegie, or American Book Award is outstanding in plot, theme, character, and style and thus is a book not to miss. Only a few books each year receive awards, so this list is a limited, but fairly sure guide.

(3) Children like them. Some are children we know. Some are the children who vote for the children's choice awards. When a book is in its twenty-seventh printing, that is a kind of popular vote from children, too. We try to indicate which books are children's favorites.

(4) We have known the book to meet a particular need. It has stimulated learning, helped someone to grow, or provided a new insight on a problem.

(5) The book is a good example. It furnishes a kind of standard by which to measure other books of the same genre—picture books, Bible stories, Christmas resources, fantasy, or fiction.

In addition to the basic bibliographic information, you will find after each book the following:

(1) Awards the book has received.

(2) The kind of book—fantasy, picture book, fiction, etc.

(3) The book audience. Publishers and reviewers usually suggest age levels for books based on such things as subject matter, reading ability, and attention span. We do not suggest a target age, since we think that all ages will find these to be good books. We list the youngest age at which the story may be appropriate, not the only age that will be interested in the book. Our age groupings are P, K, and Grades 1, 2, 3, 4, 5, 6, but these are merely guides. Children who are accustomed to books usually respond to reading those in a higher age range. Listening in a family group usually raises the level, too. Matching age and reader does not guarantee interest, but it does provide a starting point for selection.

(4) Page numbers, or unp. (unpaged), because sometimes the length of the book will be a determining factor in the choice to order it or seek it out.

(5) Audio-visual information, when we have used it with a book. FS means filmstrip.

Almost all of the books in this bibliography are available in paperback, and are in print now. Even while you read this, several new books will be born and several will pass from the list of books in print. Most of them will be available in a public library or through interlibrary loan for several years to come.

Throughout our conversations about literature we have used children's books as examples. Most of these are annotated in "Books for All Ages" or found in the "Enduring Favorites." A few books and authors that we have used as examples are missing from the bibliography because they duplicated a style, theme, or example we thought was clearer in another book. A few of the books were negative examples. We have included a list of those we omitted at the close of "Books for All Ages" in case you want to read and judge them for yourself.

11
Books for All Ages

1. Adoff, Arnold. *Black Is Brown Is Tan.*
Illus. by Emily Arnold McCully. New York: Harper and Row, 1973. Picture book, pictures essential. Rhymed. P-Gr. 2. 31 pp.

Summary, themes, and values: The brief, rhythmic text and illustrations show an interracial family enjoying and celebrating life together. The book affirms physical differences, common needs, and feelings that all races share.

2. Alexander, Lloyd. *The Prydain Chronicles.*
New York: Holt, Rinehart and Winston. Five books of fantasy, based on Welsh legends. Stories are related but independent. Excellent for reading aloud; be sure to practice Welsh names in advance. Gr. 3/4.

> *The Book of Three.* 1964. 217 pp.
>
> *The Black Cauldron.* 1965. Awards: Newbery, 1966. 224 pp.
>
> *The Castle of Llyr.* 1966. 201 pp.
>
> *Taran Wanderer.* 1967. 256 pp.
>
> *The High King.* 1968. 285 pp. Awards: Newbery, 1969; National Book finalist, 1969; American Book finalist, 1969; American Book (Paperback), 1981.

Summary: The *Book of Three* introduces us to the orphan Taran who longs to be a hero. His chance to test himself comes when Arawn, Lord of Evil, sends the Horned King against King Math and the Sons of Don. *The Black Cauldron* and *The Castle of Llyr* continue the struggle between Good and Evil and expand the cast of characters as Taran gathers a diverse group, The Companions, to serve the High King Math. Taran sets out to find his parentage in *Taran Wanderer* so he can ask the hand of Princess Eilonwy in marriage, and in the process discovers the meaning of identity. Finally, in

The High King Taran faces the Lord of Evil, Arawn. When he learns his origin he must make an important choice that reveals the nature of the true hero.

Themes and values: Action-filled, humorous, and almost a running commentary on Judaeo-Christian values. Some main ideas: the hero is one who strives for others more than for self; heroism takes many forms, physical courage being only one; recognizing and naming evil is the basis of conquering evil; we are never self-sufficient; our choices make a difference; we form our identity through choices to sacrifice for something beyond ourselves; it is in facing challenges that we become adequate to meet them; memory or history is essential to identity. The last chapter in each of the first four books summarizes the wisdom Taran has gained. Read and compare with biblical wisdom literature. Use to stimulate summaries of wisdom, rather than knowledge, gained during the year. The Book of Three, The Cauldron Born, the Mirror of Llunet, and the Truthful Harp are imaginative symbols with Christian counterparts. Taran's final choice offers insight into Philippians 2 and the Incarnation.

3. Anderson, Leone Castell.
The Wonderful Shrinking Shirt.
Illus. by Irene Trivas. Niles, IL: Albert Whitman, 1983. Picture book, pictures essential. Brief text. P. unp.

Summary: Father buys a beautiful purple-and-yellow-striped shirt which shrinks when it is washed, so it goes to Mama until it is washed again and then it goes to. . . . Its final use is quite satisfying.

Themes and values: the sharing of family life. Use with older groups as a light way to emphasize recycling.

4. Armstrong, William H. *Sounder.*
Illus. by James Barkley. New York: Harper and Row, 1969. Awards: Newbery, 1970; Lewis Carroll Shelf, 1970; Mark Twain, 1972; Nene, 1973; Sue Hefly, 1976. Realistic fiction, rural south, 1900. Based on a true experience. Gr. 4/5. 116 pp. Group or individual reading, about two hrs.

Summary: The story of a Black sharecropper family; of social and individual injustice; of a Black boy who refused to be conquered by either hate or evil, who gained courage through stories of Bible journeys, and of a great coon dog, Sounder, who embodies all that is best in an animal-human friendship. When the boy's father is taken to prison for stealing food for his hungry family, Sounder is shot and left to die. The survival of the dog who waits for his master and the long, heart-breaking search of the boy for his father and his own manhood make an unforgettable, deeply moving tale.

Themes and values: In Ch. 4, humiliation suffered without "a mumblin' word"; in Ch. 6, the discussion of Bible journeys, especially those of Joseph and David; in Ch. 8, a final expression of faith in the Shepherd God. Why do these Bible stories speak continuously to the human heart in so many situations? A way to introduce Bible study.

5. Avi. *The Fighting Ground.*
New York: J. B. Lippincott, 1984. Realistic fiction, American Revolutionary War. Gr. 5. 157 pp.

Summary: The glamour and glory of war appeal to thirteen-year-old Jonathan. He can hardly wait to fight and does not understand why his father will not let him go. However, through an unexpected turn of events, for one brief twenty-four-hour period, he does fight, is taken prisoner by three Hessian soldiers, and finds his understanding of war and life changed forever.

Themes and values: War makes life cheap, but in actuality life is wonderful and precious. Good background material for units in conflict-resolution and/or peacemaking. Also raises questions about what is *worth* fighting and dying for.

6. Babbitt, Natalie. *The Devil's Storybook.*
Illus. by author. New York: Farrar, Straus, Giroux, 1974. Ten short folk tale-like stories. Gr.

4/5. 101 pp. Any story can be read or told in five to ten minutes.

Summary: The Devil is a proud, conniving, frequently inept tempter in these tales. He is outwitted when he offers wishes, tempts to greed, or tries to capture beauty. He wins the day when he encounters pride or prejudice.

Themes and values: Some serious questions about the nature of evil, art and moral goodness, temptation, and work are raised in a light and witty manner. The story "Perfection" is a jewel for parent groups.

7. _____. *Tuck Everlasting.*
New York: Farrar, Straus, Giroux, 1975. Awards: ALA Notable Books, 1975; Christopher (Children's Book category), 1976; IBBY, 1978. Realistic fantasy beginning in the 1880s. Gr. 3/4. 139 pp. Read aloud or individually. About two hours, group discussion.

Summary: When Winnie Foster decides to run away and meets Jesse Tuck, strange things begin to happen. A kidnapping, a murder, and a jailbreak follow in swift succession. But this is not what the story is about, for Winnie faces the choice of living forever in a finite world and the Tucks help her see what this choice means.

Themes and values: A thought-provoking statement about death, explaining the cycle of living and dying that is the fate—and blessing—of this earth. Read in connection with Paul's view of death both as a conquered enemy and a doorway to "be with the Lord." In Ch. 12 Tuck speaks of death in the context of time and space. An excellent discussion starter for Gr. 6–adult.

8. Bailey, Carolyn Sherwin. *Miss Hickory.*
Illus. by Ruth Gannett. New York: Viking, 1946. Awards: Newbery, 1947. Modern fantasy. Gr. 4/5. 123 pp.

Summary: Miss Hickory is a twig doll with a very hard hickory nut for a head. She is left behind when the house is closed for the winter. With spirit and hard-headed stubbornness she survives the winter, and in the spring, by losing her head, becomes something more.

Themes and values: Miss Hickory may remind you of someone you know. The story shows great appreciation for country life. Ch. 9, about Christmas in the barn, is an excellent Christmas reading.

9. **Bierhorst, John (translator from Aztec).**
Spirit Child.
Illus. by Barbara Cooney. New York: William Morrow, 1984. Picture book. P. and up. unp. The first modern translation of the Nativity story that was written for the Aztec Indians in the mid-1500s by the missionary Fray Bernardino de Sahagún.

Summary: The text uses short paragraphs and dialogue in the Aztec tradition and is accompanied by beautiful paintings that preserve the flavor and tradition of Mexico's heritage. Drawing mainly from the accounts of Jesus' birth found in the gospels of Matthew and Luke, the story also includes bits from the legends and myths of the Aztecs and remnants of European folklore. The language is poetic and moving: "Oh spirit, O child, you are the flame, you are the light of the almighty father."

Themes and values: The Christmas story spans centuries and cultures and comes with new freshness in this retelling. Reemphasizes God's caring for all people everywhere.

10. **Bishop, Claire Huchet.** *Twenty and Ten.*
As told by Janet Joly. Illus. by William Pène du Bois. New York: Viking Press, 1952. Awards: Child Study, 1952. Realistic fiction based on actual event in France, World War II. Gr. 2. 76 pp. Read aloud in about an hour. Some background about rationing may be necessary for children.

Summary: Sister Gabriel and her twenty pupils hide ten Jewish children from the Nazis at their school in the country. During the Sister's absence, the Nazis come to search for the Jewish children. Suspense mounts as the captain, promising oranges and chocolates in exchange for information, questions the youngest child. Two Bible stories, the flight into Egypt and the miracle of the loaves and fishes, figure in the satisfying conclusion to this story.

Themes and values: An appropriate choice during Epiphany. Good readers theater possibility for mixed age group. Friendship, providence, and miracles are discussion subjects that may grow from this.

11. ———. *Yeshu, Called Jesus.*
Illus. by Donald Bolognese. New York: Farrar, Straus, Giroux, 1966. Gr. 3/4. 97 pp.

Themes and values: The boyhood of Jesus, related to the Old Testament story and the book of Acts. Excellent background; direct Bible quotations are incorporated into the text skillfully and are italicized. A very fine, sensitive recreation of these unknown years. A good example of biblical "fiction," that is, details not specifically mentioned in the Bible.

12. **Blos, Joan W.**
A Gathering of Days: A New England Girl's Journal, 1830–32.
New York: Charles Scribner's Sons, 1979. Awards: Newbery, 1980. American Book (Children's Books), 1980. Realistic, historical fiction based on a thirteen-year-old girl's diary. Gr. 5. 144 pp.

Summary: In her journal Catherine records the daily life and the changing seasons in a home firmly grounded in faith. Her mother is dead and she keeps the house, cares for her younger sister, goes to school, and shares confidences with her best friend Cassie. She faces a difficult choice when a runaway slave asks for help, a difficult adjustment when her father remarries, a dreadful sorrow when Cassie dies. In faith she faces another change as she goes to Boston to continue her schooling.

Themes and values: Like Ecclesiastes, Catherine's diary reflects the rhythm of life, a time for planting and reaping, laughing and mourning, living and dying. Each stage is accepted with faith. Catherine's difficult choice between obedience to her father's firm belief in respect for law and the needs of the slave is good for discussion. Journal keeping can be an important form of spiritual growth. Use this at the first of the year to stimulate both recall and some form of recording. A good gift for upper elementary and early junior high girls.

13. **Blume, Judy.**
Are You There God? It's Me, Margaret.
Englewood Cliffs, NJ: Bradbury, 1970. Awards: Golden Archer, 1974; Young Hoosier, 1976. Realistic contemporary fiction. Gr. 6. 149 pp. Very popular. Spanish translation. Blume says her books are a personal conversation between her and the young reader.

Summary: Margaret Simon worries about typical early adolescent problems: Will she have any friends in her new school? Why is she so flat-chested? Will she be the last girl in the class to begin a menstrual period? Will she ever have a boyfriend? She also struggles with some problems peculiar to a home where her parents, a Jewish father and a Protestant mother, have given up any reference to religion in order to avoid conflict.

Margaret is spoiled by her Jewish grandmother and badgered by her narrow, unyielding Christian grandparents. With this unpromising background Margaret still talks over most of her problems with God.

Themes and values: Identity, mixed marriages, peer relationships. Some of these natural, honest conversations with God are good examples of prayer for upper elementary and junior high students. Margaret's search for a religion is also a valuable incident for study in parent groups. Chs. 8, 15, 19, and especially her letter in Ch. 24 are the key sections.

14. **Bond, Felicia.** *Four Valentines in a Rainstorm.*
Illus. by author. New York: Thomas Y. Crowell, 1983. Very small picture book. P. unp.

Summary: One year it rains valentines, and Cornelia Augusta picks up four. She thinks carefully about which ones will be appropriate for four good friends and then sends them off. It never rains valentines again, but that is not the end of Cornelia's sending valentines.

Themes and values: A charming little book about gift-giving that emphasizes the thought over the gift.

15. **Boston, L. M.** *A Stranger at Green Knowe.*
Illus. by Peter Boston. New York: Harcourt, Brace, World, 1961. Awards: Carnegie, 1962. Realistic fiction set in England after World War II. Gr. 4/5. 158 pp. Outstanding style.

Summary: The story begins in Africa near the Congo River. Here a family of gorillas live a life of freedom and order until white hunters come. A young gorilla named Hanno is captured and sent to the London Zoo. Here, a decade later, another mistreated and misplaced creature—young Ping, a Chinese refugee—sees Hanno at the zoo and feels immediate empathy. Ping spends the summer at Green Knowe, near London, in a remarkable old house with an equally remarkable hostess. Hanno escapes and comes to Green Knowe. His friendship with Ping leads to a bittersweet ending.

Themes and values: Wonder and beauty of animals; the predatory nature of modern man, seen in the lives of animals and children; a painful picture of what it means to be caged, literally or by circumstance; the meaning of loneliness and courage; a strong appeal to love and care for all God's creation.

16. **Bridwell, Norman.** *Clifford the Small Red Puppy.*
Illus. by author. New York: Scholastic, 1972. Picture book, pictures are essential. P. unp. Almost a cartoon. Very popular.

Summary, themes, and values: Once Clifford was the runt of the litter, so small he was not expected to live through the winter. Emily Elizabeth chose him because he needed her and she loved him. She told him so one night, and then Clifford began to grow. Now he is two stories high and the hero of several other books about a big red dog.

17. **Brooks, Bruce.** *The Moves Make the Man.*
New York: Harper and Row, 1984. Awards: Newbery Honor, 1985. Realistic fiction. Gr. 6. 280 pp.

Summary: When Jerome Foxworthy "integrates" a junior high school in Wilmington, N.C., one might expect a story of racial tension. Instead, we have an exploration of an unusual friendship, of two personalities, one highly integrated and one not, and of the complexities of integrity. Jerome comes from a strong matriarchal, fatherless family; Bix comes from a family where the mother ends up in a Duke Hospital psychiatric ward. The game of basketball becomes the arena and focus for a story about coping with life.

Themes and values: It is important not to fool oneself, to understand that what one does and the way one does it affect oneself as well as others. Good picture of strong Black family life.

18. **Brown, Marcia.** *Stone Soup: An Old Tale.*
Illus. by author. New York: Charles Scribner's Sons, 1947. Awards: Caldecott Honor, 1948. Picture book; a folk tale set in a French village. K. unp. A Weston Woods FS with narration.

Summary: Two soldiers, returning from the war, trick some fearful and greedy villagers into sharing food—to the benefit of everyone.

Themes and values: A good emphasis for stewardship, the importance of each contribution. Some reasons people do not contribute.

19. **Brown, Margaret Wise.** *The Dead Bird.*
Illus. by Remy Charlip. Reading, MA: Addison-Wesley, 1958. Picture book. K. unp.

Summary: Some children find a dead bird and bury it. The story is that simple, but in the process death is faced and accepted and the importance of ritual is demonstrated.

Themes and values: A helpful book for the young child in home or church school class who has little concept of death and initial fears about the subject.

20. ———. *Goodnight Moon.*
Illus. by Clement Hurd. New York: Harper and Row, 1947. Picture book, rhymed. P. 30 pp.

Summary, themes, and values: A going-to-bed classic for the very young. A child says goodnight to everything in the room and beyond. Bedtime, security in routine, child's sense of ritual.

21. ———. *The Runaway Bunny.*
Illus. by Clement Hurd. New York: Harper and Brothers, 1942. Picture book, pictures essential. Animal story. P. unp.

Summary: When Bunny thinks about running away from home and seeking independence, his mother understands and reassures him. He cannot escape her love. The drawings illustrate the ambivalence of venturing forth versus safety and security. Though the bunny may escape, he cannot escape his mother's love.

Themes and values: Desire for independence, the unconditional and seeking nature of love. Children have fun discovering the bunny and mother in each picture. A classic for home and preschool classes. Use with youth when talking about the nature of love.

22. **Bruna, Dick.** *Christmas.*
Illus. by author. Trans. by Eve Merriam. Garden City, NY: Doubleday, 1969. Picture book, rhymed. P. unp.

Summary, themes, and values: A first book about Christmas with simple, uncluttered pictures, each figure distinct, little perspective. A good example of a picture book for the young. Because of the size and shape it needs to be placed on a table or held in a lap.

23. **Bulla, Clyde Robert.** *Daniel's Duck.*
Illus. by Joan Sandin. New York: Harper and Row, 1979. Contemporary fiction, easy reader. K. 64 pp.

Summary: Daniel decides to carve a duck for the fair. His brother, and then the people at the fair, all laugh at it. It takes a stranger to help Daniel see the true value of his work, and then Daniel, in turn, is free to answer with uncalculating generosity.

Themes and values: Encouragement for the artist in all of us; affirmation of individual worth. A

sense of self-worth enables us to act in love toward others. Let your beginning reader read this to the family or group. Bulla has a number of worthwhile stories just beyond the beginning reader level. Check his titles.

24. **Burch, Robert.** *D. J.'s Worst Enemy.*
Illus. by Emil Weiss. New York: Viking, 1965. Fiction set in rural south during the depression. Gr. 3/4. 142 pp.

Summary: D. J. Madison has trouble with his family and friends. He picks fights with everyone, cannot stand to be teased, blames other people for his problems, and finds himself increasingly isolated from his family. Two acts bring the situation to a climax. First, he throws a corncob at his little brother Renfroe, who is annoying him with animal imitations, and an infection develops that may require the amputation of Renfroe's leg. Next he maliciously causes his sister Clara May to lose a ten-dollar prize for packing the most peaches. D. J. must face himself and make a choice.

Themes and values: Read for class discussion individual chapters that illustrate the consequences of selfishness, the necessity to see ourselves honestly, the happiness of being a part of and contributing to the family and community.

25. ———. *Ida Early Comes over the Mountain.*
New York: Viking, 1980. Awards: ALA Notable, 1980; *Globe-Horn,* 1981. Fiction, rural southern mountains. Gr. 1. 145 pp. *Christmas with Ida Early* is a sequel.

Summary: Ida Early appears from nowhere to be the housekeeper/babysitter in the motherless Sutton household. Her appearance, wild exaggerations, and lax attitude about chores mark her as an unusual person, but her cooking, friendship, imagination, and humor bring joy to a bereft home. The Sutton children's loyalty is put to the test when their schoolmates first see Ida Early. Note especially the chapters "Schoolyard" and "The Letter."

Themes and values: Asking forgiveness, appreciating persons who are different, seeing beyond appearances, friendship, peer pressure.

26. ———. *Queenie Peavy.*
Illus. by Jerry Lazare. New York: Viking, 1966. Awards: Jane Addams, 1967; Child Study, 1966; George G. Stone, 1974; Georgia, 1971. Realistic

fiction, rural south, Depression. Gr. 5/6. 159 pp. Chapters divide into seven reading sessions of about thirty minutes each.

Summary: Queenie not only chews tobacco, she can spit accurately. She is a troublemaker in the eighth grade, a troublemaker to the courts. Pride and hostility are her protection against a respectable community. She idolizes her father, who is in prison, and cares little for her spiritless mother. When her father comes home and violates his parole, she must face reality. Just as he has chosen, so must she, for she is responsible for deciding what kind of person she will be.

Themes and values: Personal responsibility, giving up illusions, accepting help in our struggle to become. Queenie's situation gives insight into why she feels and acts as she does without depriving her of the dignity of responsibility.

27. ———. *Renfroe's Christmas.*
Illus. by Rocco Negri. New York: Viking, 1968. Realistic fiction about D.J.'s younger brother. Gr. 2/3. 59 pp.

Summary: The approach of Christmas seems to intensify the selfish streak that eight-year-old Renfroe is developing. He spends his time thinking about what he will get. When his father gives him the money to buy knives for himself and his brother, he spends most of it on his own knife. It seems the Christmas angel on the smokehouse door turns away each time he walks by. On Christmas night at the church program he finally offers a genuine gift—his finest present to a boy who can never say "thank you."

Themes and values: This is that rare book, a Christmas story that is not contrived or overly sentimental. We see loving family relationships, the consequences of self-centeredness, familiar rationalization for what pleases us. If a short summary of the story is given as introduction, the next-to-last chapter, "The Story Acted Out," may be read in about twenty minutes.

28. **Burningham, John.** *Mr. Gumpy's Outing.*
New York: Holt, Rinehart and Winston, 1970. Awards: Kate Greenaway, 1971; *Globe-Horn* (Illus.), 1972; Children's Book Showcase, 1972; *New York Times* Best Illustrated, 1971. Picture book, fiction; pictures essential and idyllic. P. unp.

Summary and values: A cumulative tale for the very young that illustrates language and story style to perfection. Mr. Gumpy is going for a boat ride and the animals ask, one at a time, if they may come along.

29. **Burton, Virginia Lee.** *The Little House.*
Illus. by author. Boston: Houghton Mifflin, 1942. Awards: Caldecott, 1943; Lewis Carroll Shelf, 1959. Pictures essential, more important than text at first. P. 40 pp.

Summary and values: Picture book story of a house in the country, gradually surrounded by a town. Children need help with the concept of time, seasons, change.

30. **Byars, Betsy.** *The House of Wings.*
Illus. by Daniel Schwartz. New York: Viking, 1972. Awards: National Book finalist, 1973. Contemporary fiction. Gr. 3/4. 142 pp.

Summary: As the youngest of eight children, Sammy has lived life in rural Alabama much as he pleases. Then his parents decide to look for work in Detroit and, without consulting Sammy, drop him off in Ohio with a grandfather he has never known. The house is dirty, dilapidated, and filled with birds that come and go at will. Grandfather is as strange and unkempt as the house. Angry with his parents and his grandfather, Sammy runs away, is pursued by his grandfather, and is finally diverted from his determined flight when the two discover a wounded crane. The book covers a twenty-four-hour period in which Sammy loses his self-concern in his concern for the crane and begins to see the old man in a new light.

Themes and values: Maturity through compassion; appreciating old age and those who seem different; the worth of life and the created world; responsible stewardship of the world. Ch. 4 describes the confrontation between the angry boy and the old man who loves the bird. The grandfather tells Sammy why he cares about birds. The section is worth reading aloud in any study of the created world and man's dominion over it. Excellent for camp rest periods.

31. ———. *The Summer of the Swans.*
Illus. by Ted CoConis. New York: Viking, 1970. Awards: Newbery, 1971. Contemporary fiction. Gr. 4/5. 142 pp.

Summary: Everything about Sara seems wrong to her—her feet, her hair, her orange sneakers, and her family, especially her family. Her sister Wanda and her aunt argue; her father is irresponsible; her brother Charlie is retarded. Then Charlie disappears and Sara learns what it means to care more about someone else than yourself. An imagined enemy joins in the search, and Sara learns to say "I'm sorry." Her father disappoints her once again, but she learns to accept him as he is.

Themes and values: A child who is different is seen as uniquely valuable; unselfish love is a doorway to growth; being accepted by others helps us accept ourselves. A positive picture of early adolescence and insight into the feelings and problems of those years.

32. Cameron, Eleanor. *Julia and the Hand of God.*
Illus. by Gail Owens. New York: E. P. Dutton, 1977. Fiction, California, 1923. Gr. 5/6. 168 pp.

Summary: Eleven-year-old Julia lives with her mother and brother in her grandmother's home. Her family history, her grandmother's theology, and her own actions lead her to think about how the world works and the part God plays in it.

Themes and values: Julia's questions and actions are a paradigm of a maturing child developing a world view.

33. Caudill, Rebecca. *A Certain Small Shepherd.*
Illus. by William Pène du Bois. New York: Holt, Rinehart, Winston, 1965. Awards: Clara Judson, 1966. Realistic contemporary fiction, Appalachia. Gr. 1. 48 pp. Story can be read or told without pictures, but at one point in the story the picture is important. About thirty minutes to read or tell.

Summary: With a loving and patient father to help him, mute Jamie adjusts to school and silence. Then he has a part in the Christmas pageant as a shepherd, and life takes on a new excitement. The pageant is cancelled because of a snowstorm, but Christmas comes to Jamie's barn and with it comes the miracle of speech.

Themes and values: A Christmas story of beauty and simplicity. For family reading, intergenerational gatherings, a good pre-Christmas gift.

34. ———. *Did You Carry the Flag Today, Charley?*
Illus. by Nancy Grossman. New York: Holt, Rinehart, Winston, 1966. Awards: Sue Hefly, 1974. Fiction, Appalachian mountain setting. P. With some editing can be read in a thirty-minute session. 94 pp.

Summary: In the Little School the highest honor of the day is to carry the flag at the head of the line to the school bus. Charley, just beginning school, has high hopes of the honor. Each day Charley's family asks, "Did you carry the flag today?" Each day the answer is "no." Then Charley discovers something even more valuable than carrying the flag.

Themes and values: A supporting family with confidence in Charley and without criticism of his mistakes; teachers who encourage growth through acceptance and emphasis on strength; a growing sense of what is truly valuable; and a positive picture of an impoverished area. Good preparation for the kindergarten teacher to read.

35. Charlip, Remy.
Harlequin and the Gift of Many Colors.
Illus. by Burton Supree. New York: Parents' Magazine, 1973. Awards: Irma Simonton Black, 1974. Picture book/fable. Gr. 1/2. 42 pp.

Summary: Harlequin has no costume to wear to the Carnival until his friends share, each offering a small bit of material from his or her own. The result is the symbol of love and joy, a multicolored, diamond-patterned costume.

Themes and values: The Carnival celebrates the beginning of Lent. The story emphasizes giving rather than giving up, the sum of our giving being greater than our individual gifts. A good introduction to a cooperative work such as banner-making.

36. Christopher, John. *The White Mountains.*
New York: Macmillan, 1967. Awards: George G. Stone, 1977. Fantasy with overtones of *1984* and *Brave New World.* Gr. 5/6. 184 pp.

Summary: The "capping" that takes place when young people reach puberty is a totalitarian society's way of offering security and tranquillity in exchange for obedience and conformity. Some escape, at high cost, to the White Mountains. This is the story of Will and his companions who take the risk of freedom and its attendant hardships.

Themes and values: Freedom is costly; conformity and unquestioning obedience to the existing order are not the highest values. The freedom of conscience to obey God's will, a basic tenet of protestantism, is a continuous challenge to our political and social decisions. An excellent vehicle for exploring the freedom to dissent.

37. Cleary, Beverly. *The Ramona* Series.
All published by New York: William Morrow. Beverly Cleary received the Laura Ingalls Wilder Award in 1975.

Beezus and Ramona. Illus. by Louis Darling. 1955. 159 pp.

Ramona the Pest. Illus. by Louis Darling, 1968. Awards: Georgia, 1970; Nene, 1971; Sequoyah, 1971; Young Reader's Choice, 1971, 192 pp.

Ramona the Brave. Illus. by Alan Tiegreen. 1975. Awards: Golden Archer, 1977; Mark Twain, 1978. 190 pp.

Ramona and Her Father. Illus. by Alan Tiegreen. 1977. Awards: *Globe-Horn,* 1977; IBBY (text), 1980; Garden State, 1980; Nene, 1979; Newbery Honor, 1978; Texas Bluebonnet, 1981. 186 pp.

Ramona and Her Mother. Illus. by Alan Tiegreen. 1979. Awards: American Book (Children's Paperback Fiction), 1981. 208 pp.

Ramona Quimby, Age 8. Illus. by Alan Tiegreen. 1981. Awards: Newbery Honor, 1982. 190 pp. Realistic, episodic fiction. K. Good for children just graduating from beginning readers; good for reading aloud.

Summary: Ramona first appears at nursery school age and she is seen through the eyes of Beezus (Beatrice) her older sister. She is a constant trial to Beezus, who finally comes to recognize the distinction between liking and loving on a particularly trying day. Ramona comes into her own as the pest, struggles into kindergarten, adapts as her mother goes to work, and as her father loses his job and changes careers. She must overcome night-time fears, jealousy, a sense of rejection, and insecurity, all felt with the intensity of a growing child. Life is a constant struggle, but a good and satisfying one.

Themes and values: Parents and any persons concerned for children in the life of the church should read this series. It is a course in child development. It is also a picture of a strong family. The parents are loving, encouraging, fair, and fallible. Their partnership has no rigid divisions of labor and is an expression of mutual support. There are scenes of humor, discipline, forgiveness, frustration, and joy. Ch. 7 in *Ramona and Her Father* is good Christmas reading.

38. Cleaver, Vera and Bill. *Where the Lilies Bloom.*
Illus. by Jim Spanfeller. New York: J. B. Lippincott, 1969. Awards: National Book finalist Children's Book category), 1970; *Globe-Horn,*

1970. Fiction, North Carolina Great Smokies, Gr. 5. 174 pp.

Summary: Fourteen-year-old Mary Call Luther promises her dying father that she will keep the family together, not let her older "cloudy-headed" sister marry Kiser Pease, not accept charity. With exceptional courage and tenacity she tries to carry out his wishes, supporting the family through "wildcrafting"—harvesting plants and roots with medicinal properties for pharmaceutical companies. Her struggle to keep the family together is no more difficult than her struggle to admit that, in some instances, she has been wrong.

Themes and values: Fidelity, both human and divine; pride in family name; a demonstration of hope; the natural world as a sign of God's sure promises; a positive picture of an impoverished yet rich cultural area. The parts on wildcrafting are particularly noteworthy. There is much humor in what is essentially a stark, challenging situation. Mary Call's expressions of despair and hope (143–44) have a universal quality.

39. Coerr, Eleanor.
Sadako and the Thousand Paper Cranes.
Illus. by Ronald Himler. New York: G. P. Putnam's Sons, 1977. Fiction based on an actual event following World War II. Gr. 3/4. 64 pp.

Summary: Sadako approaches the Celebration of Memory, honoring those killed at Hiroshima, and the class track race with the same zest and vitality until the day she shows the symptoms of the bomb's legacy, leukemia. A classmate brings her a folded paper crane, reminding Sadako that a thousand cranes will grant her highest wish. The story traces Sadako's valiant effort to fold the thousand cranes and the impact of her courage on her classmates.

Themes and values: The universal wish for peace; the high cost of war; appreciation of Japanese people and culture. A good opportunity to explore our symbol of peace, the dove representing the Holy Spirit. Paper-folding fits in well with this for Gr. 4 and up.

40. Cohen, Barbara. *The Binding of Isaac.*
Illus. Charles Mikolaycak. New York: Lothrop, Lee, Shepard, 1978. A richly illustrated interpretation of Genesis, Ch. 22. Gr. 3/4. unp.

Summary and values: The story is told by Isaac as an old man to his grandchildren. A personal viewpoint on this difficult story showing imaginative faith but little embellishment. Good for adults as well.

41. Cohen, Miriam. *Born to Dance Samba.*
Illus. by Gioia Fiammenghi. New York: Harper and Row, 1984. Realistic contemporary fiction set in Brazilian shantytown. Gr. 4/5. 149 pp.

Summary: Maria Antonia is sure she will be Queen of the Carnival because she can dance Samba as no other eleven-year-old in Rio. Her friend Nilton, her family, and even her rival Teresinha listen to her exuberant boasts. Then a series of events—her brother is lost, her grandmother becomes ill—tests the importance of her dream and shows her how to be a winner even when she loses.

Themes and values: Maria Antonia is a delightful heroine who embodies the vitality and strength of an impoverished group in another culture. Her bargain with the saints when her grandmother becomes ill is typical of an erroneous idea about God. Her realization that community and family are more important than personal triumph comes without diminishing her lively, flamboyant spirit.

42. ———. *No Good in Art.*
Illus. by Lillian Hoban. New York: Greenwillow, 1980. Picture book. K/l. unp.

Summary: Jim is suffering from too much art instruction so he thinks he cannot paint a picture. His classmates and a sympathetic teacher help him change his mind.

Themes and values: This is a typical problem for children who move from absolute confidence in preschool into comparisons and self-consciousness in elementary school. The accepting teacher and class are good models for children and adults. *First Grade Takes a Test* by this author portrays another elementary school problem well.

43. Cole, Joanna, comp.
A New Treasury of Children's Poetry: Old Favorites and New Discoveries.
Illus. by Judith Gwyn Brown. Garden City, NY: Doubleday, 1984. 224 pp.

Summary, themes, and values: This collection of over two hundred poems has something for everyone. Emily Dickinson, Walter de la Mare, Robert Louis Stevenson, Edward Lear, Christina Rossetti, Shel Silverstein, Ogden Nash, Langston Hughes, Randall Jarrell, e.e. cummings, and David McCord are only a few of the poets represented. The groupings are: First Poems of Childhood; People and Portraits; Animal Fair; Silly Time; Come Play with Me; When I Went Out to See the Sun; Celebrate the Time; A Different Way of Seeing; Inside Myself. The last section is a good resource to give adults the perspective of a child.

44. Collier, James Lincoln, and Christopher Collier.
My Brother Sam Is Dead.
New York: Four Winds, 1974. Awards: National Book finalist, 1975; Newbery Honor, 1975. Realistic historical fiction. Gr. 5/6. 215 pp.

Summary: The story highlights the conflict and ambivalence felt by many colonists between the ideals of the American Revolution and loyalty to England and the King. Sixteen-year-old Sam Meeker steals his father's gun to fight for freedom; his father finds that the cost is too high, the principle too slight. But it is Tim, the younger brother, who must finally live with what war does.

Themes and values: The cruelty and destruction of war; responsibility for and service to others as true courage and maturity. Fantasy gives us a clear choice between Good and Evil; real life seldom does. Older readers may began a discussion here on the ethics of war, the individual versus the collective good, and the place of individual conscience. Parts of Chs. 1 and 2 will be sufficient to set the stage.

45. Cooper, Susan. *The Dark Is Rising* series.

Over Sea, Under Stone. Illus. by Margery Gill. New York: Harcourt, Brace, World, 1965. 252 pp.

The Dark Is Rising. Illus. by Alan E. Cober. New York: Atheneum, 1973. 216 pp. Awards: *Globe-Horn,* 1973; Carnegie commended, 1974; Newbery Honor, 1974.

Greenwitch. Illus. by Michael Heslop. New York: Atheneum, 1974.

The Grey King. Illus. by Michael Heslop. New York: Atheneum, 1975. Awards: Carnegie commended, 1976; Newbery, 1976; Tir-na-n'Og, 1976.

Silver on the Tree. New York: Atheneum, 1977. Awards: Tir-na-n'Og, 1978.

Description: Fantasy. Gr. 3/4. A mixture of realism and the supernatural as the Arthurian legend is revisited.

Summary: A crumbling parchment map found in an attic in Cornwall where three children are spending a summer holiday sets them on a quest for a relic which contains a secret source of goodness and finally results in another round of the ancient war between good and evil. Allegorical and mystical, but moving forward with plenty of action, mystery, tight plot, and fine characterization. The next four books continue with other elements of the search, other tests to be met, other battles to be fought. Each of the stories is steeped in myth and ancient folklore. Those who enjoyed the Prydain Chronicles will be delighted to move on to Susan Cooper, and vice versa. In this case there is a mixing of past and present, and the protagonists are modern-day English children.

Themes and values: The struggle between Good and Evil; the idea of the remnant. Like Taran in the Prydain Chronicles, Bran is a kind of Christ-figure, the king who renounces kingly privilege and life everlasting in a distant but perfect kingdom, who throws in his lot with humankind to live, work, suffer, and share the fate of the earth's people. With this decision goodness re-enters the world forever; the possibility of Evil's winning is vanquished. Evil still exists because people are both good and bad, but it can be controlled by acts of will and conscious decisions to work for Good. The longest and hardest task of all is left to those who inherit the world "in all its perilous beauty"; they will share in the final conquest of Light. Another idea elaborated in *Greenwitch* is the mindless, unallied force of Nature or matter. This power must be taken into account and acknowledged as we live in a material world. The final exhortation is one of hope: Be of Good Cheer.

46. Coutant, Helen. *The Gift.*

Illus. by Vo-Dinh Mai. New York: Alfred A. Knopf, 1983. Fiction. Gr. 1/2. unp.

Summary: A young girl finds an unusual gift to give to her old friend Nana Marie who loses her eyesight.

Themes and values: An imaginative gift of oneself; a stimulus to seeing God's world.

47. Cresswell, Helen. *The Bongleweed.*

New York: Macmillan, 1973. Awards: Carnegie commended, 1974. Realistic fantasy in a contemporary English setting. Gr. 3/4. 138 pp.

Summary: Becky Finch plants a mysterious seed which her father, the head gardener of Pew Gardens, has been given by a botanist. It grows as an exotic, uncontrollable plant, threatening to smother the gardens and churchyard. There are varied reactions to this exciting and mysterious plant, and Becky and her mother and father find themselves at odds with most of their community before the matter is taken out of their hands.

Themes and values: Reactions to the Bongleweed are much like reactions to the quality of life people saw in Jesus. Though the Bongleweed is destroyed, the book closes with Becky's new knowledge: ". . . now it was a world where the Bongleweed had been, and that would make all the difference" (138). The Bongleweed as a symbol opens several areas of thought about new life, imagination, new perspectives to young people and adults. Read aloud for the style of sound and verbs as the Bongleweed grows.

Helen Cresswell is known by most young people today as the author of the Bagthorpe saga. She has written several imaginative books with multi-layered meanings, all published by Macmillan: *Up the Pier*—love as an act of letting go; *The Beachcombers*—opposed by the Scavengers who accumulate Things; and *The Night Watchmen*—still puzzling us, but hard to forget.

48. de Angeli, Marguerite. *The Door in the Wall.*

Illus. by author. Garden City, New York: Doubleday, 1949. Awards: Newbery, 1950; Lewis Carroll Shelf, 1961. Historical fiction, thirteenth-century England. Gr. 2. 121 pp.

Summary: Ten-year-old Robin is left crippled by the plague when his parents are away serving the king. He is nursed back to health by Brother Luke at the monastery, then nursed to spiritual health and wholeness as the Brothers show him "doors in the wall" through which he may go despite lameness.

Themes and values: The theme on which de Angeli bases her book is "I have set before you an open door" from Rev. 3:8. Books, crafts, learning, and using what skills we have are the doors the Brothers open to Robin. Physical limitation is a challenge; courage is more important than physical strength; everyone has an important place in God's world. Good background reading for church history.

49. DeJong, Meindert.
Journey from Peppermint Street.
Illus. by Emily Arnold McCully. New York: Harper and Row, 1968. Awards: National Book, 1969. Fiction set in Holland. Gr. 2/3. 242 pp.

Summary: Young Seibren goes with his grandfather to visit the inland aunt who lives at an old monastery with her giant, deaf-mute husband, also named Seibren. It is a journey in more than a geographic sense as Seibren encounters new experiences, fears, guilt, and forgiveness, love and kindness with the openness and ready response of a child.

Themes and values: The role of adults as both protectors and encouragers of independence; a good relationship with a grandparent who shares with Seibren and also learns from him. Using a charming argument, Seibren helps his grandfather mend a quarrel with an old friend.

50. de Paola, Tomie. *Andy: That's My Name.*
Englewood Cliffs, NJ: Prentice-Hall, 1973. Picture book. K. unp.

Summary: Everyone wants to use Andy's name to spell words, but they will not let him play.

Themes and values: The worth of even the smallest, the importance of names. Suggests the game of making words from other persons' names.

51. ———. *The Knight and the Dragon.*
Illus. by author. New York: G. P. Putnam's Sons, 1980. K. 32 pp.

Summary: A knight and a dragon anticipate combat with each other, since that is what knights and dragons do. They practice fighting separately, then meet for battle. With the help of the castle librarian they find a better way.

Themes and values: Peacemaking, the value of new information. Through vivid pictures, few words, and gentle humor, we see weapons of war turned into the equivalent of plowshares.

52. Eager, Edgar. *Half Magic.*
Illus. by N. M. Bodecker. New York: Harcourt Brace Jovanovich, 1954. Contemporary fantasy. Gr. 4/5. 217 pp.

Summary: Four children find a magic coin which grants half a wish. It takes practice to figure out how to wish for twice as much in order to get the whole wish, but eventually they master the art. The result is an eventful summer and a permanent change in their lives.

Themes and values: Mostly for fun, individual and group reading. A light-hearted reminder to wish carefully.

53. Ende, Michael. *The Grey Gentlemen.*
Trans. from German by Frances Lobb. London: Burke, 1974. Pb. Contemporary fantasy. Gr. 5/6. 238 pp. The translation is confusing in a few instances, but this does not affect the total narrative.

Summary: When the Grey Gentlemen come to town they encourage people to save time in their time bank. "Time Saved Is Time Doubled" say their advertisements, and soon the city is full of time savers who work efficiently and get twice as much done—except that no one has time for listening, playing, conversation, stories, or enjoying their work. Only Momo, a young girl, stands in the way of their plot to get all the time in the world, and the turtle Cassiopeia is her only ally.

Themes and values: What is time? How is it to be used? Can it, in fact, be saved? Managed? Emphasizes the gift of time, the relation of past, present, and future. Time, torn from its rightful owner, dies. An imaginative approach to a theme that is important to Christians who have been admonished to "redeem the time." *Tom's Midnight Garden* and, in a much lighter vein, *The Man Who Tried to Save Time*, deal with this subject. Some possibilities for New Year's and intergenerational study.

54. Estes, Eleanor. *The Hundred Dresses.*
Illus. by Louis Slobodkin. New York: Harcourt, Brace, World, 1944. Awards: Newbery Honor, 1945. Realistic fiction. Gr. 3. 80 pp.

Summary: Peggy and Maddie laugh at Wanda Petronski—at her clothes, her accent, and especially her claim of having one hundred dresses in her closet. It is only after Wanda moves away and leaves a gift for each of them that they see the truth about the outsider and themselves.

Themes and values: Judgment based on appearance; peer pressure; the burden of cruel actions that cannot be recalled. Upper elementary children use such fictional situations to examine peer relations in the light of Christ's example.

55. ———. *Rufus M.*
Illus. by Louis Slobodkin. New York: Harcourt, Brace, World, 1943. Awards: Newbery Honor, 1944. Realistic fiction, set during World War I.

Gr. 1/2. 320 pp. Episodic adventures make good single reading sessions. *The Moffats* and *The Middle Moffat* are two other books about the same family.

Summary: This is the story of a typical little boy—how he acts, what he thinks, how he grows. It covers his preschool and primary grade years. On the scale of history his achievements are small ordinary ones, but they are monumental in terms of his own growth and development.

Themes and values: Supporting, loving family life, virtues like thrift, hard work. Ch. 1 tells how Rufus learns to write his name and offers encouragement to small children mastering skills. Ch. 7 illumines the concept of providence; Ch. 11 could be a child's definition of grace. *Harriet the Spy* and *Are You There God?* provide a contrast in contemporary portrayals of the family. Leaders will gain from reading both and comparing.

56. Ets, Marie Hall, and Aurora Labastida.
Nine Days to Christmas.
New York: Viking, 1959. Awards: Caldecott, 1960. Picture book, Christmas in Mexico. K. 48 pp.

Summary and values: An introduction to the Christmas customs of the posada and the piñata, seen through the eyes of a little girl.

57. Ets, Marie Hall. *Play with Me.*
New York: Viking, 1955. Awards: Caldecott Honor, 1956; IBBY, 1956. Picture book. P. unp.

Summary: A little girl wants the animals to play with her, but she is too aggressive and frightens them away. When she learns to wait quietly, they approach.

Themes and values: Patience, gentleness, quietly waiting, opening avenues of trust. An attitude of receptivity, not dominance, towards nature; an attitude of openness to receive rather than to get or take.

58. Evernden, Marjorie. *The Kite Song.*
Illus. by Cindy Wheeler. New York: Lothrop, Lee, Shepard, 1984. Contemporary, realistic fiction. Gr. 4. 186 pp.

Summary: Because he feels he is responsible for the death of his parents, Jamie is sealed in an envelope of silence. The words of a poem about a kite flying free become both the medium and the symbol of Jamie's recovery. The poem is written

by a sympathetic young man who has time to spend with Jamie, and who sees that Jamie is not stupid, as he appears—only intensely troubled.

Themes and values: Sympathetic portrayal of both emotional and physical handicaps. Shows the power of acceptance and love.

59. Fisher, Aileen. *Out in the Dark and Daylight.*
Drawings by Gail Owens. New York: Harper and Row, 1980. 151 pp.

Summary, themes, and values: Aileen Fisher, winner of the 1978 NCTE Award for Poetry for Children, sees the small things of the world. She writes about rabbits, rocks, crickets, spiders, birds, and children with love and gentle humor. The poems are short, well suited to the attention span and interests of the young. A good resource for helping children marvel at the wonder of God as creator and God's creation.

60. Fisher, Leonard Everett.
The Seven Days of Creation.
New York: Holiday House, 1981. Awards: ALA Notable, 1981. Picture book with adapted text from Genesis. Ageless. unp.

61. Fitzhugh, Louise. *Harriet the Spy.*
New York: Harper and Row, 1964. Awards: Sequoyah, 1967. Fiction. Gr. 4/5. 298 pp.

Summary: Encouraged by her beloved governess, Ole Golly, eleven-year-old Harriet Welsch records her observations about people in a notebook. Her absorption in writing about people around her helps to fill a void created by self-centered parents who have little time for Harriet. A crisis occurs for Harriet when Ole Golly leaves; her notebook is found and read by classmates, who are outraged by her painfully accurate descriptions; and her parents insist she give up writing. Ole Golly writes Harriet a letter to help her find her way between her honest comments and her friends' feelings. Harriet's relationship with her parents remains unchanged, but her notebook is restored to her and she finds an outlet for her writing in school.

Themes and values: For parents and teachers to read because it is so popular with children—they love Harriet. The question of honesty and people's feelings is an important one as children learn to value the feelings of others. Ole Golly's letter in Ch. 15 combined with her reading about love from

Dostoievsky in Ch. 2 is good discussion material for Gr. 5/6 into high school.

62. ———. *Nobody's Family Is Going to Change.*
New York: Farrar, Straus, Giroux, 1974. Awards: Other Award, London, 1976; ALA Notable, 1974. Realistic fiction. Gr. 4/5. 221 pp.

Summary: Emma and Willie are siblings in a Black, middle-class family. Emma wants to be a lawyer; Willie wants to be a dancer. Neither of these ambitions fits in with the parents' preconceived notions of how their children should behave. Finally, with rare insight, Emma realizes that she cannot change her family's attitudes. Any changes must come from her.

Themes and values: Dealing with the expectations of others for us as well as our own. A book for parents, who can learn much about two-way communication.

63. Forbes, Esther. *Johnny Tremain.*
Illus. by Lynd Ward. Boston: Houghton Mifflin, 1943. Awards: Newbery, 1944. Historical fiction, Boston. Gr. 5/6. 256 pp.

Summary: Johnny is a cocky young apprentice to a Boston silversmith in pre-revolutionary Boston. An accident caused by an angry fellow apprentice maims Johnny's hand so that he must seek work elsewhere. Through a new friend, Rab, he becomes involved in delivering messages for Paul Revere and other colonial leaders. His handicap, his friendship with Rab, and the tragedies and challenges of the growing conflict bring Johnny to a new stage of understanding and maturity as the revolution begins.

Themes and values: Outstanding historical research involves us in facing the cost and consequences of war as well as the importance of freedom and self-government. Read with the Colliers' *My Brother Sam Is Dead* to illustrate the complexity of peacemaking, principles, and patriotism. Johnny's growth through handicap, suffering, and friendship is another strong theme.

64. Forrester, Victoria.
Words to Keep Against the Night.
New York: Atheneum, 1983. Poetry. unp.

Summary, themes, and values: A small book that fits small hands. Quiet, peaceful, comforting verses.

65. Fox, Paula. *One-Eyed Cat.*
New York: Bradbury (Macmillan), 1984. Awards: Newbery Honor, 1985. Realistic fiction, pre-World War II, New York State. Gr. 5. 216 pp.

Summary: One night Ned takes a forbidden air rifle and shoots, without thinking, at a shadowy movement beyond the barn. He later finds he has probably blinded in one eye a wild cat who lives in the woods. With the help of Mr. Scully, an elderly neighbor, Ned assumes responsibility for feeding the cat. Through many months he struggles with his guilt and remorse.

Themes and values: The book is a look at moral development, at the consequences of sin and the possibility of forgiveness. Family relationships are explored, as is the nature of goodness. Interaction between generations, especially Ned's friendship with old Mr. Scully, illustrates the mutual benefits that can occur when young and old communicate.

66. Fritz, Jean. *Homesick: My Own Story.*
Illus. with drawings by Margot Tomes and with photographs. New York: G. P. Putnam's Sons, 1982. Awards: American Book (Children's Hardback Fiction), 1983. Realistic fiction, autobiographical. Gr. 4. 163 pp.

Summary: Young Jean, born in China to parents working for the YMCA, is homesick for her grandmother whom she has never seen, for America where she has never been, for a school where she can sing "My Country 'Tis of Thee" loudly and with pride. Ms. Fritz has recreated the feelings and events of these years of growth for the fictional Jean in a turbulent, changing China.

Themes and values: The need to belong, for identity beyond one's own self. Jean's conflict over "God Save the King" is a present-day illustration of Psalm 137. Ch. 3, the story of the birth and death of her baby sister, is a poignant statement of our need to be loved for ourselves alone. The story of Lin Nai-Nai and her family in Ch. 4 and the young Chinese communist in Ch. 5 illustrate the unnecessary barriers of hate erected between people and nations in the name of ideological principle.

67. ———. *The Man Who Loved Books.*
Illus. by Trina S. Hyman. New York: G. P. Putnam's Sons, 1981. unp. History and legend combined. *Brendan the Navigator* is another legend/history combination about an Irish saint by Fritz.

Summary and values: Columba, the sixth-century missionary of Scotland, has a passion for books and reading, a love for Ireland and her bards, and devotion to the church. He has made three hundred copies of the Bible by hand. An important and neglected area in our knowledge; good for both adults and children.

68. Gág, Wanda. *Millions of Cats.*
New York: Coward-McCann [1928] 1956. Awards: Newbery Honor, 1929. Picture book classic. P. unp.

Summary and values: An old man sets out to get a cat for his wife and comes home with more than he bargained for. Continues to be one of the outstanding picture books for children.

69. Gauch, Patricia Lee.
Christina Katerina and the Box.
Illus. by Doris Burns. New York: Coward, McCann, Geoghegan, 1971. Awards: New Jersey Institute of Technology, 1971. Picture book. K. unp.

Summary: A refrigerator carton becomes a castle, a clubhouse, a car, a boat, a dance floor, and an occasion for disagreement between a mother and child.

Themes and values: Imagination, cooperative play. Children enjoy the story and are stimulated to create. Adults learn something about children, toys, and the way children play.

70. George, Jean Craighead. *Julie of the Wolves.*
Illus. by John Schoenherr. New York: Harper and Row, 1972. Awards: Newbery, 1973; National Book finalist, 1973. Realistic fiction, Alaska. Gr. 5. 170 pp.

Summary: Miyax, travelling alone across the arctic tundra, survives because she is adopted by a wolf pack. Content in her close relationship with nature, she recalls the loss of her father, the great hunter, Kapugen; her time in the white man's school when she became Julie; the intolerable arranged marriage which led her to flee. As her travel brings her and the wolves closer to civilization and danger for her beloved wolves, she yearns to live like a true Eskimo. News that her father is alive forces her to make painful choices between the new ways and the "hour of the wolf and the Eskimo."

Themes and values: Appreciation of the created world; the exploitation of nature; compromise between values of the past and the present; understanding of a different culture; a resourceful, courageous heroine; an education in natural history.

71. Graham, Lorenz. *David He No Fear.*
Illus. by Ann Grifalconi. New York: Thomas Y. Crowell, 1971.

Summary and values: Bible story told in rhythmic African folk tale style. Lorenz Graham recorded these stories as he heard them told. A reminder that Bible stories speak to all people and that all people make God's Word theirs in different and wonderful ways. *God Wash the World and Start Again* (Noah), *A Road Down in the Sea* (Exodus), *Every Man Heart Lay Down* (nativity), and *Hongry Catch the Foolish Boy* (prodigal son) are told in the same style.

72. Green, Bette. *Summer of My German Soldier.*
New York: Dial, 1973. Awards: ALA Notable, 1973; Golden Kite, 1973; Massachusetts, 1980; National Book finalist, 1974. Realistic fiction set in small Arkansas town, World War II. Gr. 5/6. 230 pp.

Summary: At twelve, Patty Bergen is an awkward, lonely, and unloved child. She is abused by a tyrannical father, unfavorably compared with her younger sister by an indifferent mother, and regarded as an outsider in a small southern community because she is Jewish. Patty finds love and acceptance from the family's Black maid, Ruth, whose own love and strength come from her Christian faith. Patty makes friends with a German prisoner of war from a nearby prison camp. This involvement brings a crisis that changes her life and makes her face her home situation with courage and honesty.

Themes and values: The struggle for identity; developing relationships; growth through suffering; the cost of hatred and prejudice. Joyce Landorff, a popular Christian writer, has borrowed Ruth's words about Patty's parents, "irregular people," to describe those who are, like merchandise in a sale, below the standard and will always be a problem to us. Both Ruth and Anton, the German prisoner, are despised by the community, but their acceptance gives Patty her sense of worth. Powerful reading for junior high through adults about the redemptive, life-creating power of Christian love and God's use of what is despised and rejected.

73. Hamada, Hirosuke. *The Tears of the Dragon.*
New York: Parents' Magazine, 1967. Picture book fantasy. P. unp.

Summary: For years the village had passed along fear and hatred of a dragon that no one has seen.

Then one day a little boy travels to meet the dragon and to invite him to his birthday party.

Themes and values: The results of openness and good expectations contrasted with prejudice and fear. An obvious but not heavy-handed lesson about relationships and peacemaking. Informal dramatic possibilities. Compare with Jesus' attitude toward Levi, the Gaderene demoniac.

74. Guy, Rosa. *The Friends.*

New York: Holt, Rinehart, Winston, 1973. Fiction, contemporary life in Harlem, N.Y. Gr. 6. 203 pp.

Summary: Edith, tough, streetwise, dirty, and poor, has decided that the immaculate Phyllisia, just recently from the West Indies, will be her best friend. Phyllisia wants none of this. When Edith saves her from a gang of their classmates, they do become friends, though secretly, for underneath it all Phyllisia is ashamed of Edith. At home, Phyllisia must cope with her sister, Ruby, her father, Calvin, and her beautiful mother, Ramona, who is dying. Through misdirected pride she betrays and abandons her friend and alienates her family. Finally, she comes to understand her need for Edith's special kind of love and Edith's need for what she can return.

Themes and values: Excellent as a picture of the forces that shape life in the inner city. Phyllisia's conversation with her mother about death and guilt, pp. 121–123, is particularly poignant and insightful. The book is universal in its exploration of pride as a barrier to love and understanding (both between Phyllisia and Edith, and between the father and his daughter).

75. Hamilton, Virginia.

Sweet Whispers, Brother Rush.

New York: Philomel, 1982. Awards: Newbery Honor, 1983; American Book finalist (Children's Hardback Fiction), 1983. Realistic fiction, though the presence of a ghost or memory removes it from our standard definition of realism. Gr. 6. 215 pp.

Summary: Tree (Teresa) has lived for years with her retarded brother, Dab, in an apartment paid for and stocked with food by her mother, M'Vy, a practical nurse, who is home only on weekends once or twice a month. It is a lonely and deprived existence for a young girl on the verge of growing up. The mysterious appearance of Brother Rush, her long-dead uncle, gives the story a haunting twist. He takes Tree on excursions into the past,

and through him she gains some understanding of the present.

Themes and values: The necessity for forgiveness; the consequences and burden of sin; the strength of family in acceptance of both good and bad; the power of goodness; understanding of the Black experience, or "Black reality," to use M'Vy's term. In spite of Tree's circumstances, there is an essentially hopeful nature to this strong story.

76. Haugaard, Erik Christian. *The Little Fishes.*

Illus. by Milton Johnson. Boston: Houghton Mifflin, 1967. Awards: Jane Addams, 1968; *Globe-Horn,* 1967; Spring Book Festival, 1967. Haugaard received the Hans Christian Andersen Medal in 1968. Realistic fiction, Italy, World War II. Gr. 5. 214 pp.

Summary: Twelve-year-old Guido struggles to survive in the bombed city of Naples. He gains strength and insight from two friends: Father Pietro, who has faith in redemption, and an old man, "Sack of Bones," who believes that the suffering of humanity is a deserved punishment. Both are killed in a bombing raid, and Guido and two young friends, Mario and Anna, leave the city for Casino. On the road they find the intensified cruelty and suffering that war brings, as well as heights of courage and kindness. Eventually, losing all he loves except Anna, Guido and the girl journey on. Guido continues to live with his mother's words, "all we need are love and strength," and refuses to hate because "it is understanding that makes the difference between us and the animals" (213).

Themes and values: The devastation of war; a code that enables one to survive; hope in the most degrading and unpromising circumstances. Guido's sense of responsibility for others is miraculous in his situation.

77. Heide, Florence Parry. *The Problem with Pulcifer.*

Illus. by Judy Glasser. New York: J. B. Lippincott, 1982. Fictional satire, picture book. Gr. 2. 54 pp.

Summary: Pulcifer does not watch television; he only reads books. Parents, psychologists, and teachers combine to treat his problem: accordingly, Pulcifer begins in the middle of the book; he reads ten pages of ads just as the story gets interesting; he keeps the book in just one place. The treatments fail, however, and Pulcifer continues his bad habit of reading.

Themes and values: A humorous, satirical comment on a current story. Goes well with curriculum evaluating TV, for discussing the basis for choosing what we do with our time.

78. ———. *The Shrinking of Treehorn.*
Illus. by Edward Gorey. New York: Holiday House, 1971. Awards: Children's Book Showcase, 1972; *New York Times* Best Illustrated, 1971. A sophisticated picture book. Gr. 2/3. 54 pp.

Summary: Treehorn is shrinking. When he tries to explain his problem to parents, bus driver, teacher, and principal they respond with what they are programmed to say: Sit up at the table; You look like another kid; We don't jump up at the water fountain; I'm here to be a pal. Fortunately, Treehorn solves his own problem before he disappears, but not before he demonstrates how little adults listen.

Themes and values: The importance of listening; adult values versus children's needs. Children enjoy the story and understand the problem. Youth and adults can learn a lesson.

79. Hoban, Russell. Books about *Frances.*
Illus. by Lillian Hoban. New York: Harper and Row.

> *A Baby Sister for Frances.* 1964. unp.
>
> *A Bargain for Frances.* 1970. 62 pp.
>
> *Bedtime for Frances.* Illus. by Garth Williams. 1960. Awards: ALA Notable, 1960. unp.
>
> *Best Friends for Frances.* 1969. 31 pp.
>
> *A Birthday for Frances.* 1968. 31 pp.
>
> *Bread and Jam for Frances.* 1964. 31 pp.
> Picture books with more extensive text. P.

Summary: The Badger family—Father, Mother, and Frances, and later little Gloria—face the problems common to many families: welcoming a new baby; helping Frances learn to go to bed, or share, or enjoy another's birthday. Frances's feelings and wishes closely resemble those of most children. She desires to be loved, to be noticed, to do what she wishes; she feels anger, fear, jealousy, and joy.

Themes and values: These books are widely known and very popular. They demonstrate good family patterns, furnish situations for children to recognize and examine.

80. ———. *The Mouse and His Child.*
Illus. by Lillian Hoban. New York: Harper and Row, 1967. Animal fantasy. Gr. 3. 182 pp.

Summary: The story begins and ends at Christmas. The Mouse and his child are wind-up toys. A terrible catastrophe sends them to the trash can where they are fished out by a tramp and set on the road to find a place for themselves. They encounter good and evil in a series of exciting adventures and finally establish a place of their own.

Themes and values: This is an allegory of life—funny, exciting, painful, hopeful. "What are we, Papa?" are the child's first words, expressing a universal question (4). The child's unquestioning love of Rat transforms his character. The Mouse father finds he cannot wind himself. "Well," said the Frog, "I don't suppose anyone ever is completely self-winding. That's what friends are for" (180–1). Mouse and his child cite the lesson of life: "simply and at all costs to move steadily ahead" (178). Good reading for family, for rest time at camp.

81. Hunt, Irene. *Across Five Aprils.*
Jacket and endsheets by Aljber John Pucci. New York: Follett, 1964. Awards: Charles W. Follett, 1964; Newbery Honor, 1965; Lewis Carroll Shelf, 1966. Historical fiction. Gr 5/6. 223 pp.

Summary: In April 1861, as events and feelings push the nation toward war, Jethro Creighton is nine years old. The rumors of war that reach his family's southern Illinois farm cause different reactions in his family: excitement and anticipation in Jethro; sorrow in his parents; division among his brothers; and fear in his sister and sister-in-law. As his older brothers leave for the war, one to fight for the south and the others for the north, Jethro assumes the responsibilities of adulthood. He works, studies when he can, and faces experiences that test his loyalty and courage.

Themes and values: Irene Hunt has written a story based on her grandfather's Civil War memories. It is an excellent example of the larger truth that emerges when facts are woven into fiction. Jethro's letter to Lincoln about the deserting soldiers in Ch. 9 is an especially good section to share with young people who struggle to find the right way as both family member and citizen. The book, in a low-keyed, factual way, is a realistic picture of war and what it does to the human spirit. Mr. Creighton's refusal to take revenge is a good example of how to end violence. Chs. 1 and 5 need to be combined to tell this part of the story.

82. Hutchins, Pat. *Changes, Changes.*
New York: Macmillan, 1971. unp. Awards: Art Books for Children, 1973; Children's Book Showcase, 1972; Spring Book Festival, 1971; *New York Times* Best Illustrated, 1971.

Summary and values: A wordless book depicting a couple of block figures rearranging blocks to meet different situations. A full-fledged story that stimulates block play; it can be enjoyed without adult help after the first time. Keep it near the block corner.

83. ———. *Titch.*
Illus. by author. New York: Macmillan, 1971. Awards: IBBY (Illustration, Great Britain), 1974. Picture book. P.

Summary and values: Titch, the smallest of three children, finally plays the most important part in a gardening project. Size looms large in children's thinking; smallness equals inferiority in many situations. To share at home or in class. *Happy Birthday, Sam* is another book on the same theme by this author.

84. Jarrell, Randall. *The Bat Poet.*
Illus. by Maurice Sendak. New York: Macmillan, 1963. Awards: *New York Times* Best Illustrated, 1964. Animal fiction/poetry. Gr. 2/3. 43 pp.

Summary: The little brown bat sleeps by night and stays awake during the day. He is unable to convince any of his bat family that the world of sunlight is beautiful and good. Alone each day and inspired by the mockingbird's songs, he begins to make up poems and share them.

Themes and values: Getting a new perspective; the rejection of good because it is new; the relationship of the artist to the community; the way to receive art. Beautiful writing, an unusual introduction to poetry. We have read this and Jarrell's *The Animal Family* to preschool children in family settings and they loved them. So suggested age does not always tell the story.

85. Juster, Norton. *The Phantom Tollbooth.*
Illus. by Jules Feiffer. New York: Random House, 1964. Awards: George G. Stone, 1971. Contemporary, humorous fantasy. Gr. 3/4. 256 pp.

Summary: Milo, bored with school and life, finds a mysterious tollbooth in his room and drives his little red car through it. He is, he discovers, in the Lands Beyond, stranded in Doldrums. Tock, the Watchdog, comes to his aid and accompanies him in his quest to restore banished Rhyme and Reason to the Kingdoms of Dictionopolis and Digitopolis.

Themes and values: Our responsibility to use our minds; the unity of knowledge; the responsible use of language; the importance of a positive and hopeful attitude. Juster pokes gentle fun at every aspect of academics and at every possible cliché. Milo's arrival at the Word Market, Ch. 3, is a good introduction to a study of communication and the importance of language. The cast of enemies—The Dirty Bird, the Gelatinous Giant, The Terrible Trivium, The Threadbare Excuse are a few—personify a number of the sins which we battle.

86. Kellogg, Steven.
The Mystery of the Missing Red Mitten.
New York: Dial, 1974. Awards: Children's Book Showcase, 1975. Picture book, pictures essential. P. unp.

Summary: A small girl has lost a red mitten. The mittens are the single spot of color on pages of black-and-white line drawings. As she retraces her steps for the day, she relives a joyful experience of creative play, then finds the lost mitten in a surprising place.

Themes and values: A joy to share with children, an excellent leadership resource to help adults see the imagination and motion of a preschool child.

87. Kent, Jack. *Clotilda's Magic.*
Illus. by author. New York: Scholastic, 1978. Picture book. P. unp.

Summary: Clotilda is a fairy godmother, but to her sorrow there is little demand for her service. Tommy is a very literal little boy without faith or imagination; Betty has both, so she sees the magic in ordinary events. This is a funny story of the meeting of these three characters.

Themes and values: A good story for the young; for the mature, an illustration of what we lose when we close our minds.

88. ———. *There's No Such Thing as a Dragon.*
Illus. by author. Racine, WI: Western, 1975. Picture book. P. unp.

Summary: Billy Bixbee finds a small, friendly dragon at the foot of his bed one day. He would like to play with the dragon, except his mother insists there is no such thing. Before the day is gone, the dragon gets the recognition he needs.

Themes and values: Unrecognized needs, problems, and people tend to become unmanageable. Kent has a number of books that focus humorously on important problems—fear, communication, self-esteem. Children enjoy them; they set the stage for discussion with youth/adult groups.

89. Kherdian, David.
The Road from Home: The Story of an Armenian Girl.
New York: William Morrow, 1979. Awards: Newbery Honor, 1980; *Globe-Horn,* 1979; Lewis Carroll Shelf, 1979; Jane Addams, 1980; American Book finalist (Children's Book category), 1980. Fictional biography/history, beginning in 1917. Gr. 5/6. 238 pp.

Summary: A happy, comfortable, secure home life, bounded by family and church, comes to an end for seven-year-old Veron when the Turks decide to deport or destroy all Armenians living within their borders. This is the story of Veron's survival and growth, both physically and spiritually. The book ends as she leaves at age sixteen for America and an arranged marriage to a husband she has not seen.

Themes and values: Hitler quoted the Turks' plan to exterminate the Armenians as support for his similar scheme for the Jews. It is a little-known, sobering story that reminds us of the real and terrible nature of corporate sin. It is a hopeful story of more than physical survival. Veron and Patty in *Summer of My German Soldier* are two heroines that combine well for a booktalk.

90. Kherdian, David, and Nonny Hogrogian.
Right Now.
Illus. by Hogrogian. New York: Alfred A. Knopf, 1983. Picture book, little text. P. unp.

Summary: Black-and-white pencil drawings, on the left-hand pages, show the past or the future. The right-hand pages, illustrated in pastels, extol the joys of the moment.

Themes and values: Creation is good; life is precious; God's providence is daily and continuous. Adults will share with children the ability to live in and savor the present moment.

91. Konigsburg, E. L. *Father's Arcane Daughter.*
New York: Atheneum, 1976. Fiction. Gr. 5/6. 118 pp.

Summary: When Winston's sister Caroline reappears after seventeen years, she changes the life of his handicapped sister, Heidi, frees him from a strange bondage to that sister, and brings his father new happiness. But is Caroline really his sister? A well-crafted and suspenseful story.

Themes and values: An excellent treatment of handicaps from the perspective of the handicapped, outsiders, and the family. Shame brings devastating results to all members of the family. The importance of a teacher for discipline and focus. Raises an issue of living with the facts or with a larger truth.

92. Krasilovsky, Phyllis. *The Very Little Boy.*
Illus. by Ninon. New York: Doubleday, 1962. Picture book, pictures necessary. P. unp.

Summary: Once there was a little boy. . . . A satisfying story of physical growth and psychosocial maturity. The print grows in size along with the child. Then one day there is a very little sister.

Themes and values: Growth as part of God's plan, in size, skill, and helpfulness. For the young to enjoy, and for adults to understand.

93. ———. *The Man Who Tried to Save Time.*
Illus. by Marcia Sewall. Garden City, NY: Doubleday, 1979. K. unp. A Westport Communication FS.

Summary and themes: What happens when you do everything faster and earlier? This is the book that tells you, and that helps children begin to think about time and its proper use.

94. Kraus, Robert. *Leo the Late Bloomer.*
Illus. by Jose Aruego. New York: Windmill, 1971. Awards: Art Books for Children, 1973. Picture book. P. unp.

Summary: Leo's mother reminds his father daily that Leo will grow at his own pace—and he does. A book of more value to parents and teachers than to children.

95. Krauss, Ruth. *The Carrot Seed.*
Illus. by Crockett Johnson. New York: Harper and Row, 1945. Awards: Spring Book Festival, 1945. Picture book, P. 22 pp.

Summary and themes: A small boy plants a carrot seed which no one believes will ever grow. His faith is rewarded by a spectacular carrot. Faith and hope in terms a child understands; God's dependable world.

96. Krumgold, Joseph. . . . *And Now Miguel.*
Illus. by Jean Charlot. New York: Thomas Y. Crowell, 1953. Awards: Newbery, 1954; Boys' Club, 1954. Realistic fiction, mountains of New Mexico. Gr. 4/5. 245 pp.

Summary: Twelve-year-old Miguel is the middle son who longs to go with the men of the family when the sheep are taken to summer pastures in the high mountains. He prays this wish to St. Ysidro, the patron saint of farmers, and his wish comes true through a dismaying event. Miguel then must struggle with the meaning of prayer and providence.

Themes and values: Family relationships; confirmation; the struggle for personal identity; prayer, providence. The book is excellent background material about shepherds, especially Chs. 4 and 5. Miguel and his older brother, Gabriel, discuss prayer and the ways prayers are answered in Ch. 13.

97. ———. *Henry 3.*
Illus. by Alvin Smith. New York: Atheneum, 1967. Fiction, suburban setting. Gr. 5/6. 268 pp.

Summary: Because of his high IQ and because his father's promotions mean his family moves frequently, Henry Lovering is a junior high loner. Now in Crestview, an affluent suburb of New York, he hopes to make friends; his father hopes to be vice-president; and his mother and sister hope for social status. Fletcher Larkin, a social and academic misfit, is the first problem Henry encounters. Then there is the unfavorable community reaction when his father's job requires him to install a bomb shelter that will protect only the Lovering family. The solution to his problem, Henry sees, is to find a way to end wars. Fletcher joins him in the search and becomes his friend in the process. A hurricane strikes the community and reveals the fragile strength of community and family relationships.

Themes and values: The problems of war and technology; false values; family relationships; friendship; finding identity; the mixture of good and bad in people revealed through crisis. Are young people concerned about the bomb? Read Henry's conversation in Ch. 5. In Ch. 12, old Mr. Larkin gives one view about the cause of war—women!—and concludes, We've got to invent "a better kind of human being" (133). Henry's discussion with his father about why goodness flourishes in time of tragedy (Ch. 18) is a way of approaching the problem of evil. Ch. 21

contains a statement about true friendship which young people understand. Discuss the meaning of Jesus as a friend in the context of this statement.

98. ———. *Onion John.*
Illus. by Symeon Shimin. New York: Thomas Y. Crowell, 1959. Awards: Newbery, 1960; Lewis Carroll Shelf, 1960. Realistic fiction, small California town. Gr. 5/6. 247 pp.

Summary: Onion John is an unlikely friend for twelve-year-old Andy Rusch, whose father owns the local hardware store, because Onion John has a curious accent, dresses out of the city dump, lives by superstitions, and has three bathtubs in his shack. Mr. Rusch is ambitious for Andy and eager to improve Onion John's standard of living, but both resist his efforts.

Themes and values: Confirmation; parent/child relations; the difficult business of helping. The communication between father and son in the last chapter is warm and delightful.

99. Kurelek, William.
A Northern Nativity: Christmas Dreams of a Prairie Boy.
Illus. by author. Montreal: Tundra, 1976. Awards: American Institute of Graphic Arts Certificate of Excellence, 1976; ALA Notable, 1976. Pictures and text are an essential combination. P. unp.

Themes and values: William dreams and tells of the nativity in Canadian settings. All ages will rejoice in the outstanding art, the testimony to the Christ's meaning for all cultures and circumstances. A gift for home and Christmas.

100. Kuskin, Karla. *Just Like Everyone Else.*
New York: Harper and Row, 1959. Pb. Picture book. P. unp.

Summary and themes: Jonathan James is just like everyone else except in one important respect. Repetition and surprise make this a favorite with children. It is a good statement of what the young enjoy.

101. Langton, Jane. *The Fragile Flag.*
New York: Harper and Row, 1984. Contemporary fantasy rich in realistic details. Gr. 3. 273 pp.

Summary: School children from every state have been asked to write to the President on "What the Flag of my Country Means to Me." When Georgie Hall is prevented by illness from including her letter along with those of her classmates, she decides she must deliver it in person. What follows is an impossible but marvelous journey down U.S. highway 1 from Concord, MA, to Washington, D.C. The journey itself becomes a panorama of contemporary America. Accompanied by her closest friends and a fragile old flag found in the attic, Georgie leads a march that swells into a children's crusade against nuclear war. The flag, which has all the magic of an enduring symbol, focuses attention on the true meaning of patriotism.

Theme and values: What the flag stands for—its fragile balance and substance, its promise, its refusal to be replaced by glitter and slogan or commandeered by one group over another—illustrates the power of symbols. Dealing with the impact of single-mindedness or focus, what Langton calls "will," the book raises questions about the force of innocence, purity of heart, if you will, in the face of complexities. It is not the standard black-and-white conflict of good against evil, but rather the questioning of rationality and pragmatism as the ultimate realities. Without moralism, the book raises questions of great moral importance. It tackles head-on the problem of nuclear weapons and therefore is unique and timely. It is saved from being a tract or polemic by Langton's skillful use of fantasy, her introduction of several motifs, her ability to move her readers to both tears and laughter—ultimately, by her sense of the ridiculous, the unthinkable, and the possible.

102. Laughlin, Florence. *The Little Leftover Witch.*
Illus. by Sheila Greenwald. New York: Macmillan, 1960. Contemporary, realistic fantasy. K. 107 pp. About an hour and a half reading time.

Summary: Felina, a small apprentice witch, is earthbound on Halloween night because her broom is broken. Lucinda Doon and her family offer Felina a home until next Halloween when she can return to her home at magic school. Felina hates people, pulls cats' tails, and eats only Black-bat Soup and Jibbers' Gizzards. Through patience, discipline, and love, the Doons work their own brand of magic on a difficult and unusual personality.

Themes and values: Love—its expression in discipline, understanding, and acceptance; its power to change and redeem. A funny, simple parallel to the covenant promises we make in the baptism of infants and the Christian nurture that follows. Grandfather's gift of his birthday in Ch. 7 and Felina's choice of a name in Ch. 12

are analogies to baptism. Excellent for family reading.

103. Lawson, Robert. *Rabbit Hill.*
Illus. by author. New York: Viking, 1944. Awards: Newbery, 1945; Lewis Carroll Shelf, 1963. Animal story. Gr. 1/2. 128 pp.

Summary: New folks are coming to the Connecticut farm, and the Rabbit family waits anxiously. The new folks could be a family with cats, guns, traps, poison gases, and boys. They could be an industrious or a shiftless family, and, as Father Rabbit says, "Good breeding and good garbage go hand in hand" (77). The new family, the story reveals, are different from any family the animals have known before.

Themes and values: Love and respect for all living things; sharing God's provisions with all; an environment of peace created by trust and generosity. Human history from the standpoint of the rabbits is a good commentary on our use of the earth. Good background reading for the study of ecology and Christian stewardship. Good for family reading, day camp rest time.

104. Lee, Virginia. *The Magic Moth.*
Illus. by Richard Cuffari. New York: Seabury, 1972. Realistic fiction. Gr. 1/2. 64 pp.

Summary: "Maryanne is going to die," says one of the Foss children at the dinner table. Maryanne is a member of a large and loving family. This is primarily the story of how Mark-O, the youngest, comes to terms with her death.

Themes and values: A Christian treatment of death; implied, but unexplored symbolism of the moth and cocoon and resurrection. Death, the funeral service, emotional reactions, and the support of family and friends are part of a story that has humor, love, and hope.

105. Le Guin, Ursula. *A Wizard of Earthsea.*
Illus. by Ruth Robbins. Oakland, CA: Parnassus, 1968. Awards: *Globe-Horn,* 1969. Lewis Carroll Shelf, 1979. Fantasy. Gr. 5/6. 204 pp.

Summary: Ged, a young boy, has a gift which must be trained and developed at the school for wizards. However, he misuses his talent and looses into the world a monstrous evil, a shadow which pursues him to the end of Earthsea. During the course of his many adventures he learns about himself and the nature of evil.

Themes and values: The reality of sin, expressed by the existence in each of us of a shadow side; life as a quest; friendship; the idea of conflict of opposites within people. The book is rich in psychological and religious symbolism: the conquest of evil through recognizing and naming it; the steadfast friend who will not abandon Ged as he flees to the end of the universe; the consequences of choosing to use our gifts selfishly.

106. L'Engle, Madeleine. *Ladder of Angels: Scenes from the Bible Illustrated by Children of the World.* New York: Seabury, 1979. 128 pp.

Themes and values: Old Testament Bible stories with poems and story-like comments by L'Engle. The pictures were submitted during the Year of the Child by children around the world. Pictures may be viewed without text. Any age will enjoy this. It is encouraging to children to see the artistic expressions of other children.

107. ———. *Meet the Austins.* New York: Vanguard, 1960. Contemporary fiction. Gr. 3/4. 191 pp.

Summary: The Austins are a close-knit family—a physician father, mother, and four children. The death of their Uncle Hal and the year-long stay of a spoiled child in their home create pressure and growth in serious and funny situations. The story is seen through the eyes of twelve-year-old Vicky.

Themes and values: A positive picture of family life, love, acceptance, and forgiveness; a positive picture of adolescents growing in understanding. Mrs. Austin's discussion of death at the beginning of the book is a sample of L'Engle's theological orientation—Christian, jargon-free, profound. *The Moon by Night* and *A Ring of Endless Light* continue the story of the Austins, the latter book containing an emphasis on psychic power, exploring the theme of real communication.

L'Engle's Newbery winner, *A Wrinkle in Time,* has gone through forty-four printings. It introduces a science fiction trilogy, each book probing theological questions as a legitimate part of an exciting story. L'Engle's books are significant resources for seeing the relation of fiction and theology.

108. Lewis, C. S. *The Chronicles of Narnia.* Illus. by Pauline Baynes. New York: Macmillan.

> *The Horse and His Boy.* 1954. 191 pp. Awards: Carnegie commended, 1955.

The Last Battle. 1956. Awards: Carnegie, 1957. 174 pp.

The Lion, the Witch and the Wardrobe. 1950. 154 pp. Awards: Lewis Carroll Shelf, 1962.

The Magician's Nephew. 1955. 167 pp.

Prince Caspian. 1951. 186 pp.

The Silver Chair. 1953. 208 pp.

The Voyage of the "Dawn Treader." 1952. 210 pp.

Fantasy set in contemporary England and the land of Narnia. Gr. 2/3.

Summary: These seven books comprise the history of Narnia, a land which is created by the song of Aslan the Lion. In *The Magician's Nephew,* even as the creation occurs, evil is at hand, brought by two English children, their magician Uncle Andrew, and a wicked Queen. Because the children's pride and jealousy have brought the Queen back to life and into the new land, Aslan decrees that the evil must be conquered by "the sons and daughters of Adam." Some time later (and Narnian time is quite different from ours), four children from London—Peter, Susan, Edmund, and Lucy—find their way through the back of a wardrobe into the country of Narnia and join Aslan in the fight against the wicked Queen who has turned Narnia into a country where it is always winter, never Christmas *(The Lion, the Witch and the Wardrobe).* Narnian history is a continuous struggle to establish good against evil in *The Horse and His Boy, Prince Caspian,* and *The Silver Chair. The Voyage of the "Dawn Treader"* adds a fifth modern English child to the story as the Prince and the children travel to the edge of the sea and dreams. In *The Last Battle* Narnia is destroyed, but the real Narnia and the children move on to the adventure of Joy.

Themes and values: The temptation in these stories is to use them to teach Christian theology. Resist this. Read them and let the stories speak for themselves. Lewis said he wrote the chapters in about equal lengths so they could conveniently be read aloud. He also said they were stories of "supposal" and not allegories, but it will be impossible to read these books as a Christian without seeing parallels and applications. Aslan, the Lion, binds the books together, and his character, how he is known, his intent for creation, and his relation to his creatures are part of each story. He embodies the Terrible Goodness, or to borrow a phrase which Lewis applied to the writings of George MacDonald, the "inexorable love" of God. Events of an exciting story are also commentaries on temptation, revelation, redemption, atonement, evil, goodness, faith, obedience, judgment, and death.

Perhaps some comment should be made about sexist stereotypes. Narnia reflects a courtly, Arthurian-like climate where girls, unless they are witches, are treated with protective courtesy. The children's conversations—and these are probably the weakest part of the books—express conventional thoughts about what girls fear and boys feel. However, females have an equal though sometimes different role in the action, and the total impression is one of neither masculine nor feminine superiority.

A sampling of themes: Narnia is created through song: *The Magician's Nephew*, Ch. 9. The salvation of the pagan, or unbeliever: *The Last Battle*, Ch. 15. Repentance and rebirth: *The Voyage of the "Dawn Treader,"* Ch. 6, 7. Temptation: *The Lion*, etc., pp. 24-31; *The Silver Chair*, Ch. 12. Atonement, redemption through sacrifice: the final chapters of *The Lion*, etc. Lucy, returning to Narnia after some time, says, "Aslan, you're bigger." The Lion replies, "That is because you are older, little one." "Not because you are?" she asks, and the Lion answers, "I am not. But every year you grow, you will find me bigger" (*Prince Caspian*, 117).

109. Lindgren, Astrid. *Lotta on Troublemaker Street.*
Trans. from Swedish by Gerry Bothner. Illus. by Julie Brinckloe. New York: Macmillan, 1963. Fiction. K. 57 pp.

Summary: When five-year-old Lotta's mother insists she wear an old sweater for play, she runs away from home to Mrs. Berg's shed next door. Here she finds what freedom from family means, and through her parents' love, the way back home.

Themes and values: Family life, saying "I'm sorry," forgiveness, steadfast love. All of us need help in restoring relationships when our actions seem unforgivable.

110. Lionni, Leo. *Frederick.*
New York: Pantheon, 1967. Awards: Caldecott Honor, 1968; *New York Times* Best Illustrated, 1967. Picture book. K. unp.

Summary: While the other field mice gather food and supplies for the coming winter, Frederick does not seem to be doing his share. But he tells them he

is working. "I gather sun rays for the cold dark winter days." Frederick is a poet.

Themes and values: Value of all different kinds of abilities; conflict caused by lack of understanding of differing gifts; need for cooperation and mutual appreciation. Pictures are an important part of the story; the text is richer than most preschool picture books. Paul's discourse on the function and value of different members of the body is well illustrated in this tale. The life of the group depends on many different contributions.

111. ——. *Swimmy.*
New York: Pantheon, 1963. Awards: Caldecott Honor, 1964; Art Books for Children, 1973; *New York Times* Best Illustrated, 1963. Picture book. K. unp.

Summary: Swimmy, a small black fish, organizes a school of equally small red fish to face the dangers of the deep water.

Themes and values: Courage and cooperation. The book is stunning, a visual stimulus to creativity, a story simple enough for the toddler.

112. Lobel, Arnold. *Frog and Toad Together.*
New York: Harper and Row, 1971. Awards: Art Books for Children, 1973; Children's Book Showcase, 1973; Newbery Honor, 1973; Spring Book Festival, 1972. Easy reader, picture/story book. K. 64 pp. Five episodes.

Summary: Toad makes a list of what he is to do for the day, then faces the problem of what to do when the list blows away, because fetching it is not on the list. Frog and Toad practice using will power with a box of cookies on the table and with very little success. Frog works hard to make a garden grow. Toad realizes that friendship is more important than acclaim. This book shows that amazing stories can be told with a limited vocabulary.

Themes and values: Justly popular with beginning readers, these books are well known by most school children. Frog's struggle to make his garden grow makes a funny introduction to Jesus' parable of the Kingdom where growth is inevitable and impressive; removing temptation is the theme of the cookie story. Children can read these stories to adults as part of a Bible study. Can be presented to a group through Miller/Brody FS version.

113. Lord, Athena V. *Today's Special: Z.A.P. and Zoe.*
Illus. by Jean Jenkins. New York: Macmillan, 1984. New York State, Greek community. Episodic fiction. Gr.3. 150 pp.

Summary: While the parents must work, it becomes the job of Zach (Z.A.P.) to watch his four-year-old sister, Zoe. How can he maintain his leadership in the neighborhood with a tagalong little sister? But Zoe is every bit a match for Z.A.P., and the book is a series of comic adventures until finally Zoe comes up with the perfect solution to end Z.A.P.'s baby-sitting problems.

Themes and values: A warm and satisfying look at Greek-American culture in 1939. Happy family relationships. Picture of quick-thinking, self-confident youngsters. The "ideal" picture of the kind of childhood that produced the adults who made America grow and prosper.

114. Lord, Bette Bao.

In the Year of the Boar and Jackie Robinson.
Illus. by Marc Simont. New York: Harper and Row, 1984. Episodic realistic fiction, New York City, 1940s. Gr. 1. 169 pp.

Summary: Before Sixth Cousin sails to America from China, she chooses the most American name she can think of: Shirley Temple. With such a name, how can she fail in her new country? This spirit of optimism pervades the story as Shirley Temple Wong goes to school, learns English, and finds that kids come in all varieties and colors. The game of baseball becomes the vehicle that helps her assimilate, make friends, and achieve. Jackie Robinson becomes a symbol of America where opportunity beckons, where it is important that each person do his best, both individually and as a member of the team.

Themes and values: Identity with one's origins, and pride and respect for ancient heritages, need not lessen appreciation for new cultures or new ways. Use as a companion piece to Jean Fritz's *Homesick,* to show the strengths of American culture and to develop the ideas of opportunity and freedom for all. The strong bonds of family are emphasized, as are the warmth and security of the Chinese-American community and the importance of friends in loving and supporting roles.

115. MacDonald, George. *At the Back of the North Wind* [1870], *The Princess and the Goblin* [1871], and *The Princess and Curdie* [1882].
Illus. by Arthur Hughes and James Allen. London: Octopus, 1979. Fantasy. Gr. 2/3. 621 pp.

Summary: At the Back of the North Wind tells the story of Diamond, a young boy who lives above a stable; Old Diamond, the cab horse for whom he was named; and the North Wind, who blows through Diamond's room and takes him across cities and seas to adventures beyond his humble home. As Diamond's love and trust for North Wind grows, he longs to go to the Back of the North Wind, but he can only reach this destination by going through, not around, the Wind.

Themes and values: Through the North Wind, MacDonald expresses a bracing concept of suffering and the apparent cruelty of God to some while others experience love and care. The North Wind, who appears as a beautiful, powerful lady, says to Diamond, ". . . you're not to call me *ma'am*. You must call me just my own name—respectfully, you know—just North Wind" (20). Diamond struggles to distinguish between dreams and reality, when neither can be grasped by reason (Ch. 36). MacDonald's fertile imagination illumines heaven, death, and life beyond death.

Summary: In *The Princess and the Goblin* the goblins mine the caves below the castle where Princess Irene lives. The goblin prince plans to capture the little princess and make her his wife, thereby reclaiming the country above ground the goblins feel is rightfully theirs. At the top of the castle, unknown to everyone but the princess herself, her great-great grandmother spins a ball of fine yarn to help Irene and the miner, Curdie, defeat the goblins.

Summary: The Princess and Curdie picks up the story several years later when Irene has gone to live in the capital of her country. The Grandmother sends Curdie on a mission to save the kingdom and rescue the princess again. Now he meets the old woman for himself and accepts the unusual assistance she offers to those she calls. The books are best read in sequence, though each is a complete story alone.

Themes and values: Merely a sampling: In the first book, Irene and her grandmother discuss names in Ch. 3; the nature of gifts in Ch. 15; faith when no one shares her experience, Ch. 22. In the second book Curdie comes to know the Grandmother through his sorrow at shooting one of her pigeons. His description of what he has done wrong is a moving prayer of confession (Ch.3). In Ch. 7 the Grandmother discusses the gift of poverty. In Ch. 8 Curdie, through intense suffering, receives wisdom that enables him to discern between good and evil. In the process he learns something about the suffering of the Grandmother.

116. ——. *The Light Princess* [1867].
Illus. by Maurice Sendak. New York: Farrar, Straus, Giroux, 1969. Awards: *New York Times* Best Illustrated, 1969. Fantasy. Gr. 2/3. 110 pp.

Summary: A curse at her christening deprives the Princess of her gravity. She floats away easily and can never shed a tear. It takes the willing sacrifice of a prince to change things.

Themes and values: A picture of life without sorrow or sympathy; the gift of crying; the power of unselfish love.

117. ——. *The Lost Princess: A Double Story.*
Intro. by Elizabeth Yates. Illus. by D. Watkins-Pitchford. New York: E. P. Dutton, 1965. Fantasy. Gr. 1/2. 142 pp.

Summary: Princess Rosamond is incorrigible, and the King and Queen summon the Wise Woman to tell them what to do. Her answer, when the parents grow angry at her comments, is to spirit the child away. In another family, Agnes is very good by her parents' standards, but to teach her true goodness, the Wise Woman takes her from the humble shepherds who are her parents. The results of the Wise Woman's training surprise both sets of parents.

Themes and values: The Wise Woman represents the "inexorable love" of God. Discipline as an expression of love; pride as the ultimate sin; growth through obedience.

A note about George MacDonald: His works could be included in the "Enduring Titles" list, as they were published in the late nineteenth century and have continued in print in several new editions for over a century. His work is not so universally known as some, but as literature of significance to the church it should come at the top of the list. He is, according to C. S. Lewis, a mythopoetic genius. A major value in his work is the personality representing God; she is always a woman, and concepts are expanded without argument over pronouns. The language and descriptive passages make the books a challenge to children today. Initially they are best shared in families; children will return to them on their own—and so will adults.

118. MacKinnon, Bernie. *The Meantime.*
Boston: Houghton Mifflin, 1984. Contemporary fiction. Racial tensions. Gr. 6. 181 pp.

Summary: The story takes place from September 27 through October 9. On September 27, a rock comes hurtling through the Parrish living room window, heralding the onrush of violence and tension in high school and neighborhood. Sides are drawn. Fear and hatred are almost out of control. In the meantime, Luke must decide how he will behave toward a white girl, toward a teacher he respects, toward his family, and toward the other Black students, especially his friend Nate.

Themes and values: Choices in a complex situation are not easy, but they must be made and should be made according to principles which stop the spread of hatred. The story shows that we can rebel against systems and structures that reinforce evil. It can help foster racial understanding and appreciation for individual merit, and it also shows that principle is costly.

119. MacLachlan, Patricia. *Unclaimed Treasures.*
New York: Harper and Row, 1984. Realistic fiction. Gr. 5. 118 pp.

Summary: Willa and her twin, Nicholas, move into a new house, make new friends, and explore the meaning of extraordinary and ordinary. This is the summer the twins' mother is pregnant, the summer three females whose names begin with W learn something about love, the summer where each one does something quite extraordinary without seeming to do so.

Themes and values: The important things in life are not always obvious. Each person has worth, depths unplumbed, capabilities unrecognized. "We are all, let us hope, unclaimed treasures" (92).

120. McGinley, Phyllis. *The Plain Princess.*
Illus. by Helen Stone. New York: J. B. Lippincott, 1945. Fiction in a folk tale style. Gr. 1/2. 64 pp.

Summary: The King and Queen despair of finding a husband for their ugly daughter, Esmeralda. Dame Goodwit accepts the task of making her beautiful, using methods anyone can try with guaranteed results.

Themes and values: Beauty is based on goodness, unselfishness, character. A good story for a society that emphasizes physical beauty, especially in girls. The obvious moral is so gently spelled out with quiet humor that it is not oppressive. Young people have fun with it too.

121. Mahy, Margaret. *The Haunting.*
New York: Atheneum, 1982. Awards: Carnegie, 1983. Contemporary fiction/fantasy. Gr. 5/6. 135 pp.

Summary: On the way home from school, eight-year-old Barney has a strange vision and hears a voice saying, "Barnaby's dead! I'm going to be very lonely." The death of his great-uncle Barnaby brings to light a peculiarity of his family history: the presence of a psychic or "magician" in each generation. Barney's place in the family comes as a surprise to himself and to the reader.

Themes and values: The use and misuse of abilities; the dynamics of family relationships. This is primarily a story about family, about finding one's rightful place in the family, about using or denying the gifts one has. Troy remarks about her great grandmother, "Her magic died, but other good things died with it because it was her own specialness she killed" (117). Psychic phenomena is a subject which is usually ignored or decried by Christians. The book may open this topic for discussion, but it is not the main theme of the book. Read for style.

122. Mathis, Sharon Bell. *The Hundred Penny Box.* Illus. by Leo and Diane Dillon. New York: Viking, 1975. Fiction. Gr. 2. 47 pp.

Summary: Great-great-Aunt Dew is one hundred years old, and she has a Lincoln penny in an old wooden box for every year of her life. Each penny prompts Aunt Dew to tell some part of her story to young Michael, the one person in the house who listens and understands her. Michael's mother wants to get rid of the hundred penny box, an eyesore taking up valuable space in a small room. Michael and Aunt Dew know that the box is crucial to the old woman's life and identity. A senile, helpless woman and a little boy join forces against a practical, well-meaning mother.

Themes and values: The hundred penny box is a strong symbol—of a personal life, of a part of Black history, of the struggle to make room for the new without destroying the old. A warm picture of a relationship between young and old; a sympathetic portrayal of the problems of the aging and of three generations in a home.

123. Merrill, Jean. *The Pushcart War.* Illus. by Ronni Solbert. New York: William R. Scott, 1964. Awards: Boys' Club, 1965; Lewis Carroll Shelf, 1965. Imaginative realism in a Runyonesque style. Gr. 4. 223 pp.

Summary: In 1976 the mammoth trucks threaten to force the pushcarts from the streets of New York. Then, after the day of the Daffodil massacre, Old Anna, Morris the Florist, and other pushcart merchants decide to fight back. Pea shooters and tacks are two of the most effective weapons in this battle of the underdog against Goliath. Ingenuity and basic wisdom win out in this funny book with serious undertones.

Themes and values: The author says that for the peace of the world we must understand how wars begin, and this fictional history makes at least one war small enough to understand. Right can win without bloodshed. We know at least one cabin of junior campers who refused to go home until the last pages of this book were read.

124. Miles, Miska. *Annie and the Old One.* Illus. by Peter Parnall. Boston: Little, Brown, 1971. Awards: Art Books for Children, 1973; Christopher, 1972; Commonwealth Club of California, 1971; Newbery Honor, 1972. Picture book, realistic fiction. Gr. 3. 44 pp.

Summary: Annie's grandmother has the Navajo understanding that there is a time for all things to return to the earth. She explains to Annie that when the rug on the loom is finished her time will be gone. Annie plots ways to keep her grandmother from weaving, until the Old One helps her see the plan and passes the weaving on to her.

Themes and values: An avenue to talking about death, here understood as a natural part of earth's cycle; a positive picture of native Americans.

125. Minarik, Else Holmelund. *A Kiss for Little Bear.* Illus. by Maurice Sendak. New York: Harper and Row, 1968. Awards: *New York Times* Best Illustrated, 1968. P. 32 pp.

Summary: Little Bear draws a picture and sends it to his grandmother; she sends him back a kiss by way of his animal friends.

Themes and values: Love multiplies and creates an atmosphere of caring and giving. Tangible expressions of affection demonstrate what can happen when we live Jesus' gospel of love. This book is for individual or small group sharing because of the small, perfect illustrations.

126. Ness, Evaline. *Josefina February.* Illus. by author. New York: Charles Scribner's Sons, 1963. Awards: Spring Book Festival, 1963. Picture book, Haiti. K. unp.

Summary: Josefina February plans to buy grandfather bright red shoes for his birthday; the gift requires a sacrifice that young children will appreciate.

Themes and values: A story of unselfish giving; a picture of Haiti, its life and customs.

127. ———. *Sam, Bangs & Moonshine.*
Illus. by author. New York: Holt, Rinehart and Winston, 1966. Awards: Caldecott, 1967. Picture book. K. unp.

Summary: Samantha has trouble telling the truth; most of her talk is just moonshine. Then one day her stories prove very harmful to her young friend, Thomas, and her cat, Bangs, and Sam learns to distinguish between truth, lies, and imagination.

Themes and values: A problem most children face as they become more verbal and also compete for attention. Lovely pictures are valuable but not essential. Good for small groups and home reading with some discussion. "Why do you think Sam called Bangs a fierce lion? Why did she say her mother was a mermaid? When is it fun to 'make things up'? When is it important to tell just what we know is true? What happened when Sam made Thomas think that what was just a story was real?"

128. Norton, Mary. *The Borrowers.*
Illus. by Beth and Joe Krush. New York: Harcourt Brace Jovanovich, 1952. Awards: Carnegie, 1953. Fantasy set in England. Gr. 5/6. 180 pp.

Summary: Where do the things go that you lay down and can never find again? The Borrowers took them, of course. These are the little folk who live under the floor boards or eaves of houses. One day the most adventurous girl borrower is discovered by the lonesome boy who spends the summer in the house. That fact and the Borrowers' ever more risky forays into the drawing room and other parts of the house cause trouble with a capital T.

Themes and values: Greed and its consequences; community; the universality of loneliness, fear, curiosity, and other basic human emotions. The Borrowers, who took more than they needed, yielded to temptation, and fell on hard times. A non-threatening way to see how unwilling we are to live by "Give us this day our daily bread." As the Borrowers become more fearful and secretive, they grow smaller. The life of the English child in this book is so different from that of any American child that reading about it is an education in itself.

129. O'Dell, Scott. *The Black Pearl.*
Illus. by Milton Johnson. Boston: Houghton Mifflin, 1967. Awards: ALA Notable, 1967;

Newbery Honor, 1968. O'Dell is the winner of the 1972 Hans Christian Andersen Award. Realistic fiction with symbolic elements; Baja, California. Gr. 5/6. 140 pp.

Summary: Ramon Salazar, now counted a man in his father's diving and pearl business, sails alone to the Bay of the Manta Diablo and there finds the perfect pearl, the Pearl of Heaven. The Pearl is considered the property of the fabled giant ray that represents the power of evil to the people of Baja, California. The pearl brings tragedy to the community, evil in the person of Gaspar Ruiz, and wisdom to Ramon, who learns we cannot trade with God.

Themes and values: The reality and conflict of good and evil, the power of greed, the motive for offering. The book has the spare, intense, heroic quality of a myth. It can be condensed to less than an hour of reading, adapts well to readers theater for an elementary-through-adult group to set the stage for stewardship season.

130. ———. *The Hawk That Dare Not Hunt by Day.*
Boston: Houghton Mifflin, 1975. Historical fiction, Europe. Gr. 5/6. 222 pp.

Summary: Smuggling was a way of life in sixteenth-century England, and some important items in this trade were religious tracts and Bible translations. William Tyndale follows his call to translate the Bible to his death. His story is told through the eyes of a young seaman who felt the impact of his personality and the power of the translated Book.

Themes and values: This is an important chapter in the history of the Bible, recreating the time, the place, and the danger of making the Bible available to all. Only two characters are fictional, the seaman and his uncle.

131. ———. *Island of the Blue Dolphins.*
Boston: Houghton Mifflin, 1960. Awards: Newbery, 1961; Lewis Carroll Shelf, 1961; IBBY, 1962; Nene, 1964; Southern California Council on Literature, 1961; William Allen White, 1963. Historical fiction based on authentic records. Gr. 5/6. 181 pp.

Summary: The raiding Aleuts force Karana's tribe to flee their island home. She leaves the ship at the last moment when her brother Ramo does not come, then year passes year as her tribesmen do not return for her. Her brother is killed by wild dogs; completely alone, she learns to live and to love her surroundings.

Themes and values: The brief outline cannot do justice to a story that continues to move upper elementary children and youth year after year. It should be read for writing style and as a witness to young people's concern for serious themes. Karana's appreciation of her world, her giving up revenge as a motive, her example of steadfast courage are all inspiring. A good way to introduce a discussion about solitude and the necessity of developing resources without reliance on others. A strong and inspiring heroine. Very popular.

132. ——. *The King's Fifth.*
Illus. by Samuel Bryant. Boston: Houghton Mifflin, 1966. Awards: Newbery Honor, 1967. Historical fiction, sixteenth century. Gr. 5/6. 264 pp.

Summary: Esteban de Sandoval awaits trial in a Spanish prison because he has deprived the king of the fifth of the New World treasure the law requires. He recalls the road that has changed him from eager mapmaker, hungry for knowledge, to a prisoner charged with theft and murder. The book's climax allows him another chance to choose an honest life with a higher purpose.

Themes and values: Destructive greed and redeeming goodness; the checkered history of Christian missionary work among the natives. A particularly powerful picture is Esteban struggling to carry loads of gold that will weight him to his death.

133. ——. *Sing Down the Moon.*
Boston: Houghton Mifflin, 1970. Awards: Newbery Honor, 1971. Historical fiction. Gr. 4/5. 124 pp.

Summary: Between Spanish slavers and American soldiers, the Navaho tribe find life in their homelands a continuous struggle to stay alive. This slice of history is told through the eyes of Bright Morning, a young Navaho girl whose tribe is forced to leave home and land and re-settle near Fort Sumner. Bright Morning persuades her dispirited and lamed husband to escape with her and return to their homelands for the birth of their child.

Themes and values: An appreciation for another way of life; an understanding of our national policies that have been cruel and unjust. "How could you have changed national policy had you lived then? What are some of the consequences of the strong treating the weak unjustly?" Young people can discuss such questions with applications to issues today.

134. Parish, Peggy. *Amelia Bedelia.*
Illus. by Fritz Siebel. New York: Harper and Row, 1963. Fiction. K. unp.

Summary and themes: Amelia Bedelia is a housemaid who takes every instruction literally. When she is told to put out the lights, she takes all the bulbs out and hangs them on the line. There are a number of Amelia books; children love them all. Language and its meanings are an important part of learning and communication. These books sharpen such understanding.

135. Paterson, Katherine. *Bridge to Terabithia.*
Illus. by Donna Diamond. New York: Thomas Y. Crowell, 1977. Awards: Newbery, 1978; Lewis Carroll Shelf, 1978. Gr. 4/5. 128 pp.

Summary: Terabithia is the secret kingdom created by two fifth graders who are loners: Jess, a rural boy from a poor family, and Leslie, a new girl, financially and educationally rich, from the city. Leslie's courage, imagination, and honesty open a new world to Jess, until the day Leslie is killed in an accident. Jess must wrestle with grief, loss, guilt, and anger as he comes to terms with this experience.

Themes and values: Friendship, family, the needs and problems of upper elementary children; death, not as a natural part of life but as a tragic interruption, and the emotions and questions that surround it. Ch. 8 contrasts the conservative religious background of Jess with Leslie's complete lack of formal belief but emotional response to the story of Easter. It frames the question "What happens when you die?" It is a book for family reading and discussion.

136. ——. *The Great Gilly Hopkins.*
New York: Harper and Row, 1978. Awards: National Book, 1979; Newbery Honor, 1979; Christopher, 1979; Garden State, 1981; Georgia, 1981; Iowa, 1981; Massachusetts, 1981; William Allen White, 1981. Fiction. Gr. 5/6. 148 pp.

Summary: Gilly Hopkins is a proud, defensive, angry, intelligent foster child who lives on the illusion that some day her mother will come to claim her. In the meantime she must put up with a stupid foster mother who loves her, a frightened retarded foster child who looks up to her, an elderly Black boarder who offers her friendship, and a Black schoolteacher who understands and challenges her. It is a dangerous situation for a girl whose main weapons are hostility and indifference.

Themes and values: The power of accepting love, displayed especially by large, simple Trotter; the life and problems of a foster child. "How did Trotter express her faith to Gilly?" is a question that leads young people into a discussion of Christian witness.

137. ———. *Jacob Have I Loved.*
New York: Thomas Y. Crowell, 1980. Awards: Newbery, 1981; American Book, 1981. Fiction. Gr. 5/6. 215 pp.

Summary: Louise Bradshaw is a twin who feels that she has missed her inheritance and identity. Her sister Caroline is sickly, and so receives more attention; is gifted musically, and so receives educational advantages; is beautiful, and so gets the boy Louise loves. At work among the oysters and crabs of Chesapeake Bay, Louise begins to find her own identity and to place her family relationships in perspective, but the process must be completed away from her island home as a nurse in a mountain community.

Themes and values: The title invites us to think about the story of Jacob and Esau; the story raises some interesting questions about who we are and why we are like we are, the burdens that are ours by birth and the burdens we make for ourselves. Louise has one interpretation of her life; the village another, expressed by one as "God in heaven's been raising you for this valley from the day you were born" (209). A good book for young people when they ask if God is fair, if God has a plan.

138. Pearce, Philippa. *Tom's Midnight Garden.*
Illus. by Susan Einzig. New York: J. B. Lippincott, 1958. Awards: Carnegie, 1959; Lewis Carroll Shelf, 1963; IBBY, 1960. Fantasy, modern England. Gr. 4/5. 229 pp.

Summary: What is the secret of time? The book begins with Revelation 10:6: "And the Angel swore that there should be time no longer." Tom is unhappy when he is forced to spend time with an aunt and uncle. His intense yearning for a playmate and a place to play propel him into someone else's dream and hence into another level of reality where past and present coexist. One night when the grandfather clock in the hall strikes thirteen he discovers both a delightful playmate

and a wonderful garden in back of the house which vanishes in the daytime. Is it all real?

Themes and values: What is real? What we can touch and feel? What can be explained and seen? Connect these questions with a basic statement about time in Christian theology and several other books about time from the bibliography. This book is considered by most critics as one of the outstanding works of juvenile literature in this century. The quotation on the clock is Rev. 10:1–6. It may send the reader to the Bible to see if the passage is merely a Victorian ornament or an accurate interpretation.

139. Peterson, Hans. *Erik and the Christmas Horse.*
Illus. by Ilon Wikland. New York: Lothrop, Lee, Shephard, 1970. Picture book, fiction set in Sweden. P. unp.

Summary: A little boy's generous spirit cements a friendship and brings a valued Christmas gift.

Themes and values: a simple story in the spirit of Christmas set in another land and culture.

140. Pinkwater, Manus. *Wizard Crystal.*
New York: Dodd, Mead, 1973. Picture/fable in almost cartoon style. K. unp.

Summary: A magic crystal at the bottom of their pool is the secret of the frogs' continuous happiness. A wicked wizard steals the crystal and wakes up to a shocking surprise.

Themes and values: A brief, provocative fable, reminding us that what we own may ultimately own us.

141. Rabe, Berniece. *The Balancing Girl.*
Illus. by Lillian Hoban. New York: E. P. Dutton, 1981. Picture book, pictures essential. K. unp.

Summary: Though confined to a wheelchair, Margaret specializes in balancing—books on her head, blocks one on top of the other. The children in school are thinking of ways to raise money at the carnival, and Margaret uses her skill to raise the most money of all.

Themes and values: A natural, unsentimental treatment of a physical handicap, a plucky and attractive heroine. Children love trying to imitate Margaret's balancing scheme; have plenty of dominoes on hand. A book to share with a small group or to have as a resource in church school class and church library.

142. Raskin, Ellen.

Nothing Ever Happens on My Block.
Illus. by author. New York: Atheneum, 1966.
Awards: Art Books for Children, 1973; *New York Times* Best Illustrated, 1966; Spring Book Festival, 1966. Picture book, pictures essential. Brief text. K. unp.

Summary, themes, and values: Chester Filbert, staring ahead in boredom, complains about his uneventful life, while all around him. . . . The pictures remind us that our narrow vision limits our life.

143. Robinson, Barbara.

The Best Christmas Pageant Ever.
Illus. by Judith Gwyn Brown. New York: Harper and Row, 1972. Awards: Georgia, 1976; Young Hoosier, 1978. Fiction. Gr. 1/2. 80 pp.

Summary: The Herdmans, the worst children in town, come to church for refreshments and stay to take part in the Christmas pageant.

Themes and values: Christmas touches the lives of these children on the fringe of society, and their interpretation helps those within the church see the truth. This book has been made into a TV special and reprinted in several magazines, so it is well known. But try reading it rather than seeing it. For family and for intergenerational Christmas gatherings. It can easily be condensed to an evening, blocked for several readers. It is fresh, funny, and touching.

144. Robinson, Veronica. *David in Silence.*
Illus. by Victor Ambrus. New York: J. B. Lippincott, 1965. Fiction set in England. Gr. 4/5. 126 pp.

Summary: David, a new boy in the neighborhood, is deaf. David's selfishness and pride cause some problems in making new friends; the neighborhood children's misunderstanding and a few instances of deliberate cruelty cause others. Both David and the children must overcome these handicaps before David can feel at home in his new surroundings.

Themes and values: A painful, unsentimental, yet positive look at deafness from the viewpoint of children who must learn to communicate and of David, who is deprived of sound and speech. The story takes one inside the experience of being unable to communicate or to reach others.

145. Rockwell, Thomas. *How to Eat Fried Worms.*
Illus. by Emily McCully. New York: Franklin Watts, 1973. Awards: Golden Archer, 1975; Iowa, 1980; Mark Twain, 1975; Massachusetts, 1976; Nene, 1976; South Carolina, 1976; Young Hoosier, 1977; Young Reader's Medal (K–3), 1975. Fiction, high comedy. Gr. 2/3. 116 pp.

Summary: As everyone knows, a dare is a dare; for fifty dollars to buy a used minibike, Billy accepts Alan's challenge: eat one worm a day for fifteen days. Billy proceeds with high ethical standards and culinary imagination; his opponents cheat and try every dirty trick possible. But Billy wins a hilarious victory through perseverance, guts—literally—and ingenuity.

Themes and values: A most popular book with children, partly because Billy is an authentic hero, breaking the mental barriers we often erect of what we can and cannot do and partly because "yucky" subjects appeal to elementary grades. A most revealing book for adults, showing us peer relationships, elementary grade taste and conversation; a family response to what is important to a child and very bizarre to them. A point to ponder: the process through which what is repugnant becomes acceptable and even desirable.

146. Scott, Ann Herbert. *On Mother's Lap.*
Illus. by Glo Coalson. New York: McGraw-Hill, 1972. Picture book, pictures essential. P. unp.

Summary, themes, and values: Mother holds Michael, his prize possessions, a puppy, and finally a baby sister on her lap, and Michael is reassured to find that there is room for all. A familiar problem for the child who fears displacement by a sibling. The charming depiction of the Eskimo home and mother, and the warm and involving illustrations, are two strengths of this book.

147. Sebestyen, Ouida. *Words by Heart.*
Boston: Little, Brown, 1979. Awards: ALA Best Books for Young Adults, 1979; International Reading Assn., 1980. Fiction, turn of the century. Gr. 5/6. 162 pp.

Summary: Ben Sills, a Black man of faith and strength, moves his family to a small west Texas town where the prejudice is less virulent and the educational opportunities are greater. Here Lena, his oldest daughter, proves her ability by winning the Bible verse memory contest, and here both

Lena and Ben must put into practice the words that she has learned by heart.

Themes and values: Living the words of the Bible; peacemaking; the cost of prejudice; the redemptive power of sacrificial love, the value of each person seen through the eyes of God. A powerful story that will challenge and enrich every young person and adult who reads or hears it. A good introduction to Bible study. The contrast between Lena who knows the "words by heart" in the Bible contest in Chs. 1 and 2, and Ben Sills who *lives* the words by heart is a sharp illustration of the difference between knowing and living God's word. Ch. 8 tells of a struggle to stand against peer pressure. Ch. 13 describes how Lena sees the words of the Bible in a new light; her struggle to save the boy who has killed her father epitomizes both the motive and the cost of peacemaking. This book should be in every church library.

148. **Selden, George.** *The Cricket in Times Square.*
Illus. by Garth Williams. New York: Farrar, Straus, Giroux, 1960. Awards: Lewis Carroll Shelf, 1963; Massachusetts, 1979; Newbery Honor, 1961. Animal story. K. 151 pp. If reading aloud, think about omitting the Chinese accent, or practice it carefully.

Summary: Unintentionally, Chester, a country cricket, arrives in New York City via a picnic basket. In the Bellinis' newsstand he makes friends with Tucker the Broadway mouse and Harry the Cat, who introduce him to life in the city. Chester's beautiful voice brings him fame and fortune and enables him to save the Bellini family from bankruptcy. This success also compels Chester to decide what is important in his life.

Themes and values: Friendship; community; the need for fulfillment. Glory and fame are not necessarily the means to happiness. Chester the Cricket does good things with his voice—even singing Italian opera—but that is not his true calling. The idea of vocation, proper use of talent, finding of one's place and purpose in life is an important theme in childhood literature. Here, it is done with rare style and good humor. The scenes between Mario and the Chinese restaurant owners are some of the most delightful in contemporary literature. Family reading, children's recreation.

149. **Sendak, Maurice.** *The Nutshell Library. Alligators All Around, Chicken Soup with Rice, One Was Johnny, Pierre: A Cautionary Tale.*
Four small books bound separately. New York: Harper and Row, 1962. An alphabet book, a book of months, a counting book, and a story. Sendak won the Hans Christian Andersen Award in 1970. P.

Themes and values: The books are well-known favorites. We include them in teacher training events to illustrate interests and preferences of the preschool child, and occasionally to remind the indifferent not to be like Pierre.

150. ———. *Where the Wild Things Are.*
Illus. by author. New York: Harper and Row, 1963. Awards: Caldecott, 1964; Art Books for Children, 1973, 1974, 1975; Lewis Carroll Shelf, 1964; IBBY, 1966; *New York Times* Best Illustrated, 1963. Picture book. Illustrations must be shared. P. unp.

Summary: Max is sent to bed without his supper because he raises a rumpus. In his bedroom his fantasy takes him to an imaginary kingdom where he becomes King of the Wild Things and calms them with his stare. He returns from this journey to his bedroom where he finds his dinner "still hot."

Themes and values: Wild things are present in our lives, even in the lives of the very young; control of the wild things hinges upon looking them in the eye. The continuing popularity of this book speaks of children's struggle for self-control, the recognition of their divided nature, their need for security, the assurance of a safe return after forays into wild places "where someone love[s you] best of all."

151. **Seuss, Dr. [Theodore S. Geisel].**
And to Think That I Saw It on Mulberry Street.
New York: Vanguard Press, 1937. Awards: Lewis Carroll Shelf, 1961. Rhymed picture book. P. 61 pp.

Summary, themes, and values: Seuss books are known by virtually every child who has any contact with books. Wise adults will ask why this book and the following are so popular with children. In some instances, because they are so familiar, the books furnish a widely known analogy or reference point in teaching and preaching.

152. ———. *The Cat in the Hat.*
New York: Random House, 1957. Limited vocabulary reader, rhymed humorous fantasy. P. 61 pp.

Summary, themes, and values: Mother is out; the Cat in the Hat comes to visit two children and wreaks havoc while they watch with a mixture of alarm and fascination. This is one of the initial easy readers that all first graders and many kindergarteners read to themselves.

153. ———. *Horton Hatches the Egg.*
New York: Random House, 1940. Awards: Lewis Carroll Shelf, 1961. Picture book, humorous fantasy, rhymed. P. unp.

Summary, themes, and values: Horton the Elephant takes over nest-sitting for an irresponsible bird named Maisie. Through storm and danger he is faithful "one hundred percent," and fidelity receives its just reward. Making and faithfully keeping promises are central in our understanding of God and in our relationship with others. This is a lighthearted example of a serious topic. *Horton Hears a Who* (New York: Random House 1954) is story of this same faithful elephant's protecting a populace too small to be seen, because "after all, A person's a person no matter how small."

154. **Sharmat, Marjorie Weinman.**
A Big Fat Enormous Lie.
Illus. by David McPhail. New York: E. P. Dutton, 1978. Picture book, pictures essential. Gr. 1/2.

Summary: The narrator denies taking the cookies and now he is stuck with a lie that assumes tangible form, gradually growing larger and more menacing. He chooses honesty with evident relief.

Themes and values: Why is telling a lie bad? What does it do to us? This is an attempt to answer the question in a funny, graphic way. Younger children, who seem to be the natural audience, may take the story too literally. Older elementary and youth may laugh, but will find it a starting point for discussing the burden of falsehood.

155. ———. *The 329th Friend.*
Illus. by Cyndy Szekeres. New York: Four Winds, 1979. Picture book. P. unp.

Summary: A raccoon who must always have company around invites enough friends to dinner to insure a crowd and learns who his best friend really is.

Themes and values: Loving ourselves is part of our Christian faith; growing in solitude is an important part of maturing. Children enjoy the crowded pictures; young people and adults can react to the idea.

156. **Silverstein, Shel.** *Where the Sidewalk Ends.*
New York: Harper and Row, 1974. Illus. by author. Poetry. In some cases illustrations are essential. P. 166 pp.

Themes and values: Subject matter is wild and wonderful—unicorns, boa constrictors, gypsies, and giants, as well as garbage, band-aids, and love. The poems are frequently wise, occasionally profound, and always fun. Most are narratives. These, as well as those in *A Light in the Attic*, are dearly loved by preschool and elementary children. "Merry . . ." is a sad commentary on the faded Christmas spirit, "Lester" is Everyman who wants much and enjoys nothing, and "Jimmy Jet" depicts the sad fate of a TV watcher. A book to enjoy with all ages.

157. **Singer, Isaac Bashevis.** *Stories for Children.*
New York: Farrar, Straus, Giroux, 1984. Original fiction, partly autobiographical. Pre–World War II, Polish, Jewish culture. Gr. 2. 337 pp.

Summary, themes, and values: This collection of stories written by the Nobel laureate transcends its Jewish, Polish background with all the universal appeal of folklore. Every story has charm and something to offer. Many of the stories describe biblical customs and elaborate on old Bible stories. "The Wicked City," for example, describes Sodom and speculates about Lot and his family. The "Power of Light" is a lovely story about hope and faith. The stories about "Schlemiel" are truly funny, especially "When Schlemiel went to Warsaw" and "The Day I Got Lost." The last chapter, "Are Children the Ultimate Literary Critics?", tells how Singer feels about children, about writing for them, and about the function of literature.

158. **Sonneborn, Ruth.** *Friday Night Is Papa Night.*
Illus. by Emily A. McCully. New York: Viking, 1970. Picture book. P. unp.

Summary, themes, and values: A Puerto Rican family worries because Father is late, then welcomes him. We see the love, warmth, and pleasure in small material gifts that characterize good family life in any circumstances.

159. **Southall, Ivan.** *Let the Balloon Go.*
Illus. by Ian Ribbons. New York: St. Martin's, 1968. Awards: Australian Children's Book Council commended. Fiction. Gr. 4/5. 142 pp.

Summary: A spastic child is left alone when his over-protective mother must be gone for the day. He determines that he will use his freedom to climb a tree, reach the top, and say "Hi-ya" to God. The simple story has almost unbearable suspense.

Themes and values: An admirable hero, an enlightening portrayal of the hopes and needs of those with physical limitations, a reminder that all young people need the freedom to make choices and take risks.

160. ———. *The Sword of Esau.*
Illus. by Joan Kiddell-Monroe. New York: St. Martin's, 1968. Gr. 4/5. 116 pp.

Themes and values: Jacob, Gideon, and Jonah re-told. The stories of Jacob and Gideon are good examples of drawing together considerable material, remaining fairly close to Scripture, and adding detail and dialogue that stir imagination without claiming to be history. The informal, colloquial style makes these good guides for storytelling.

161. Speare, Elizabeth George. *The Bronze Bow.*
Boston: Houghton Mifflin, 1961. Awards: Newbery, 1962; IBBY, 1964. Historical fiction set in New Testament times. Gr. 5/6. 254 pp.

Summary: The purpose of Daniel Bar Jamin's life is to destroy the Romans who are responsible for his parents' deaths and his sister's precarious physical and emotional health. The book's title comes from Ps. 18:34 and 2 Sam. 22:35: "He trains my hands for war, so that my arms can bend a bow of bronze." Daniel works and waits, first as part of a zealot band and then with a group of young guerillas, for God to avenge his enemies. His hatred threatens his sister's life, embitters a friendly Roman soldier, and endangers his friends. Finally through his friend, Simon the Zealot, he meets Jesus, who shows him that hate can never bend the bronze bow.

Themes and values: Excellent New Testament background, fiction that is rich in detail without the Hollywood epic mentality. A moving statement about the cost of hatred, the power of love, the way to peace, and the personality of Jesus. Recommended for church libraries, for individual or group reading.

162. Spier, Peter. *Noah's Ark.*
Illus. by author. Garden City, NY: Doubleday, 1977. Awards: Caldecott, 1978; Art Books for Children, 1979; Lewis Carroll Shelf, 1978; Christopher, 1978; IBBY, 1980; *New York Times* Best Illustrated, 1977. Picture book, introductory poem. K. unp.

Themes and values: This is not just a picture book for the young. There are details and perspectives here that make it sophisticated enough for adults. Note the sexist concept that women fear mice. A Weston Woods FS with music and animal sounds is available for group viewing.

163. Steig, William. *Yellow and Pink.*
New York: Farrar, Straus, Giroux, 1984. Picture book. K. unp.

Summary: Two small figures, one painted yellow, one pink, find themselves lying in the sun one day. What ensues is a discussion about how they got there, whether or not anyone made them, or whether they were made by accident.

Themes and values: A provocative discussion that lays out the basic contentions of those who believe life was "created" and those who believe it evolved by accident. The resolution suggests in favor of creation, but leaves the element of mystery. Worth looking at.

164. Sutcliff, Rosemary. *The Lantern Bearers.*
Illus. by Charles Keeping. New York: Henry Z. Walck, 1959. Awards: Carnegie, 1960. Historical fiction. Gr. 5/6. 252 pp.

Summary: The time is the end of the Roman Empire in Britain. Aquila and Flavia, Roman siblings whose family have lived in Britain for centuries, owe allegiance to Rome but love the land that has bred them. When the last legions pull out of Britain, Aquila makes the difficult choice to stay in the land of his birth. He has barely returned to his family before his father is killed, his sister is captured by raiding Saxons, and he himself is captured and taken as a slave by marauders from Scandinavia. The cruel life and struggle for survival of brother and sister until their paths cross again brings a little-known and dark period of history to life.

Themes and values: New life out of destruction; the remnant that keeps the best of the past alive; a pattern in the great sweep of history; the individual life related to a larger scheme.

165. Taylor, Mildred D. *Roll of Thunder, Hear My Cry.*
Frontispiece by Jerry Pinkney. New York: Dial, 1976. Realistic fiction, South, 1930s. Awards: Newbery, 1977; *Globe-Horn* (Fiction Honor), 1977; National Book finalist, 1977; Young Reader's Choice, 1979. Gr. 5. 276 pp.

Summary: The Logans are one of the few Black families in Mississippi who own their own land. They struggle to keep that land in the face of white hatred and racial prejudice. Cassie, at nine, and her three brothers learn about injustice, integrity, and self-respect as their parents organize a boycott against a storeowner who has cruelly murdered a Black man.

Themes and values: A thoughtful exploration of some of the underlying causes of racial prejudice, with a specific look at the historical Black/white relationships of the Deep South. The book shows that people of goodwill have always existed; though at times their numbers have been too small to have effect, nevertheless they persist in living by their convictions—sometimes at great price.

166. Thurber, James. *The Wonderful O.*
Illus. by Marc Simont. New York: Simon and Schuster, 1957. Gr. 2/3. 72 pp.

Summary: A villainous pirate has banished the letter O from an island because his mother was once wedged in a porthole. When the islanders find and use four words with O—love, valor, hope, and freedom—the pirate is overcome.

Themes and values: Four key words in our faith and what life is like with and without them. The story can be followed by early elementary children, but the play on words is sophisticated and appropriate for upper elementary. Thurber's other fantasy/fairy tales contain this same combination of wordplay, humor, and goodness. *Many Moons* with its outstanding illustrations is a Thurber fantasy suitable for younger grades. All of this author's works are a joy to hear, but reading them aloud well requires practice.

167. ———. *The Thirteen Clocks.*
Illus. by Marc Simont. New York: Simon and Schuster, 1950. Fantasy/fairy tale. Gr. 3/4. 124 pp.

Summary: The cast of characters in this tale includes a wandering minstrel/prince, Zorn of Zorna; a bewitched princess, Saralinda; a wicked Duke who lives in a castle where time is frozen; the Golux; and the Todal that "looks like a blob of glup" (50). The predictable ingredients of a fairy tale are all here—dungeons, jewels, quests, dangers, and spells, but arriving at "happily ever after" is a unique experience of sound and symbols.

Themes and values: A primary value in Thurber's works is its sound and poetry. Cold, frozen time, the absence of tears and laughter suggest the nature of evil. The fantasy closes with practical advice from the Golux for the young lovers. "Keep warm," he said. "Ride close together. Remember

laughter. You'll need it even in the blessed isles of Ever After" (120–1).

168. Tolkien, J. R. R. *The Hobbit.*
Boston: Houghton Mifflin, 1938. Awards: Spring Book Festival, 1938. Fantasy. Gr. 4/5. 317 pp.

Summary: Hobbits are small, respectable, home-and-comfort-loving people who live in Middle Earth. Bilbo Baggins is somehow led by Gandalf the Wizard into doing very unexpected and uncomfortable things—like facing a dragon, goblins, Wargs, and the Gollum; travelling afar; and searching for treasure. In the process Bilbo finds courage and a significance to his life that he had not suspected.

Themes and values: This is the prologue to Tolkien's *Lord of the Rings* trilogy. In the writings of Tolkien the interests of youth and adults have found a meeting place. Courage, sacrifice, faith, and a purpose greater than the individual life are all here. The capacity for both good and evil is clearly seen in the struggle to retrieve the treasure. You will look long before you find a more chilling figure of Evil than the Gollum. Family and group reading, an introduction to one of the great fantasies of this century.

169. Turkle, Brinton. *Obadiah the Bold.*
Illus. by author. New York: Viking, 1965. Picture book, fiction, colonial Nantucket. K. unp.

Summary: Obadiah Starbuck is inspired by his brass spyglass to be a pirate, until play with his brothers and sisters shows him the consequences of a lawless life. His father shows him some ways to be brave and bold that are more in keeping with his family's Quaker tradition.

Themes and values: The expression of true courage; a good picture of Quaker life. Illustrations add much to the story. A book to share with young children in small groups, to read at home.

170. Uchida, Yoshiko. *The Birthday Visitor.*
Illus. by Charles Robinson. New York: Charles Scribner's Sons, 1975. Fiction, Japanese-American household. Gr. 3/4.

Summary: Emi is sulking because a visitor, a minister from Japan, is coming on her birthday. Courtesy to guests is a high priority in her home, but she hates to share her day. The visitor is a happy surprise, despite a funeral that must be conducted.

Themes and values: A home where love is expressed in gentle discipline, a good relationship between a minister and a young child. Simply a good story.

171. Udry, Janice May. *Let's Be Enemies.*
Illus. by Maurice Sendak. New York: Harper and Row, 1961. Picture book. P. unp.

Summary, themes, and values: Two little boys quarrel and make up. Children recognize the situations and responses and can talk about the causes of enmity and friendship. Adults will see what bothers children, their emotional intensity, their quick changes and readiness to forgive and forget. Except we become as children. . .

172. Untermeyer, Louis, comp., ed., with Intro. by author. *A Time for Peace: Verses from the Bible.*
Illus. by Joan Berg Victor. New York: World, 1969. unp.

Themes and values: Selected from the King James Version, primarily poetry. A vital theme, an important exercise—to read and listen to the Bible as poetry. A good selection.

173. Viorst, Judith.
Alexander and the Terrible, Horrible, No Good, Very Bad Day.
Illus. by Ray Cruz. New York: Atheneum, 1972. Awards: Georgia (Picture Book), 1977. Picture book. K. unp.

Summary, themes, and values: Alexander's trials are enjoyable to children, enlightening to adults. The emotional reaction to a prizeless cereal box, the keen sense of injustice when an accusation is false, the feeling of persecution when one must sit in the middle without a window—these loom large in the life of the small. *I'll Fix Anthony,* dealing with sibling rivalry, captures the feelings of the young with the same ring of truth.

174. Voigt, Cynthia. *Building Blocks.*
New York: Atheneum, 1984. Contemporary fantasy, set in 1974. Gr. 3. 128 pp.

Summary: Brann Connell resents his father, Kevin, because he thinks he is a "loser," a passive, unaggressive figure who is unwilling to take charge of his own life. He seems to accept whatever happens with a shrug of his shoulders and the answer, "It's fate." For example, Kevin could sell the farm he has inherited to help pay the tuition for his wife to go to law school, but he is unwilling.

Getting away from a scene of tension, Brann escapes to the basement and falls asleep in a building block fortress. The blocks are old, handmade ones that have been passed down from father to son. When Brann awakes, he finds himself moved thirty-seven years backward in time where he encounters his own father as a child. What he learns in a single day of adventure and challenge results in a more mature and understanding ability to cope with life in the present.

Themes and values: The New Testament admonition to "judge not" assumes new meaning when we see Brann encounter the people and environment that shaped his father's life. Societal changes and attitudes are depicted by the movement back in time. The definition of courage expands as we experience Kevin's demand for truth unvarnished by excuses or rationalization. The story recognizes that strength can be an inner quality, not always manifested outwardly.

175. Waber, Bernard. *Ira Sleeps Over.*
Illus. by author. Boston: Houghton Mifflin, 1972. Awards: Children's Book Showcase, 1973. Picture book. K. 48 pp.

Summary: Ira is invited to spend the night next door with Reggie. Shall he take his teddy bear named Tah Tah? Parents and sister offer advice, while Ira worries about what Reggie's reaction to Tah Tah will be.

Themes and values: Our common frailties; the wisdom of being ourselves; the desire for others to think well of us and the fear of ridicule, concerns which are common to all ages.

176. Waldron, Ann.
The Integration of Mary-Larkin Thornhill.
New York: E. P. Dutton, 1975. Awards: ALA Notable, 1975; New Jersey Institute of Technology, 1977. Fiction. Gr. 5/6. 137 pp.

Summary: What happens when you want to belong to the most popular crowd in school and your father is a minister whose stand on integration is unpopular? You find yourself away from the crowd and the only white student in an all-Black school. The Thornhill family faces one crisis after another with humor, home-baked cookies, and faith.

Themes and values: Faith at work in the world; the example of parents with convictions who ask something of their children and support them as they ask; a picture of early adolescence and peer relationships; a segment of history that should be remembered.

177. Wallace-Brodeur, Ruth. *Callie's Way.*
New York: Atheneum, 1984. Contemporary fiction. Gr. 5. 119 pp.

Summary: Callie's Way is funny and fresh. Being a minister's daughter plus the "different" one in a family where excellence is expected, Callie may find growing up a little more difficult than most children do. The boys she used to play ball with now ask her to dance. She is not sure if she is ready for that. Then she meets Megal in the Crane Home for the Aged. And Callie knows she is going to grow up all right, but she is going to do it "her" way.

Themes and values: A story about good family relationships with the normal tensions compounded by adolescence. Callie is delightful and realistic. Her family and friends are recognizable and sympathetically presented. This is an on-target vignette of the ambivalences and complexities most youngsters deal with as they seek to establish their own identities. It is a moving picture of an intergenerational relationship.

178. Walsh, Jill Paton. *Fireweed.*
New York: Farrar, Straus, Giroux, 1969. Awards: Spring Book Festival, 1970. Realistic fiction, World War II. Gr. 6. 133 pp.

Summary: Bill meets Julie in an air raid shelter during the London Blitz of 1940. He is fifteen; she is close to the same age. Since both are homeless and without adult protection, they join together to survive on their own. While eluding authorities, who will send each off to places they do not want to go, the children spend a brief time together that becomes a period of resourcefulness and ingenuity, of character testing, and finally of pain and disillusionment, as naïveté yields to the hard facts of reality.

Themes and values: Growing up, the persistence of everyday life and happiness even during periods of stress and death; the bonding, unifying qualities between people in times of danger. The book shows the waste and destruction of war; the unity and comradeship that come from sacrificing together for another person. The end gives an understanding of the pain of rejection, and the healing that can result.

179. Wangerin, Walter, Jr. *The Book of the Dun Cow.*
New York: Harper and Row, 1978. Fantasy. Gr. 5/6. 241 pp.

Summary: In the days before time or people, Chaunticleer the Rooster rules his portion of the world wisely and well. The animals are keepers of a benign order in the world above, but beneath, Wyrm lives imprisoned, struggling to be free. The confrontation between these symbols of light and dark provides the momentum and the plot of the story.

Themes and values: An allegory of good and evil, sacrifice and redemption; an understandable explanation of God's help and presence in time of grief. The end of the book illustrates the necessity for sacrificial action and the reconciling effects of such action. Perhaps best shared in a read-aloud situation because of the heroic tone and complexity of the language.

180. Wenning, Elisabeth. *The Christmas Mouse.*
Illus. by Barbara Remington. New York: Holt, Rinehart, Winston, 1959. Picture book, combination of animal story with historical basis. K. unp.

Summary: "Silent Night" was written for the Christmas Eve service in the Oberndorf church because the organ was not working. Father Mohr and organist Gruber collaborated on this beloved carol from necessity—a necessity created by the church mouse, Kaspar.

Themes and values: The facts are accurate; Kaspar, of course, is imaginary, but his delightful role makes this good family reading at Christmas, or good entertainment at any Christmas gathering. Pictures are valuable but not essential.

181. White, E. B. *Charlotte's Web.*
Illus. by Garth Williams. New York: Harper and Row, 1952. Awards: Lewis Carroll Shelf, 1959; Newbery Honor, 1953; George G. Stone, 1970; Surrey School Book, 1972. Animal story. Realistic country life. Gr. 2/3. 184 pp.

Summary: Wilbur is Fern's pet pig, but the realistic demands of farm life mean that Wilbur must be sold and eventually become bacon. Charlotte is a spider who lives in Wilbur's barn, travels to the state fair with him, and by sacrificial effort guarantees his survival.

Themes and values: This is the book where the taste of children, critics, and teachers meet. It has been real aloud to virtually every school class in middle America. Wilbur's expanding horizons to include others, the varied friends he makes in the barn, the sacrifice of Charlotte and her ultimate death, and Wilbur's adjustment to life without her—all of these themes are developed with artistic skill.

182. Wier, Ester. *The Loner.*
New York: David McKay, 1963. Awards: Newbery Honor, 1964. Fiction, Montana. Gr. 5/6. 153 pp.

Summary: Boy travels with migrant workers from place to place. He is nameless, abandoned early in life and forced to make his way in the world. When his only friend is killed in a tragic accident, he runs blindly away and is found, nearly dead, by Boss, an equally lonely shepherdess whose only son has been killed by a bear. Home is a special word to a loner, and through the winter months, Boss's trailer and sheep herd come to represent home to Boy, who chooses David for his name.

Themes and values: The meaning of home, both physically and spiritually; of names; of family and belonging. Boy's comments about the biblical David are found on pages 46–48. The shepherd background is good supplementary material for church school.

183. Wilder, Laura Ingalls. *The Little House* Series.
Illus. by Garth Williams. New York: Harper and Row, 1953.

> *By the Shores of Silver Lake.* 1939. 291 pp. Awards: Newbery Honor, 1940; Young Reader's Choice, 1942.
>
> *Little House in the Big Woods.* 1932. 238 pp. Awards: Lewis Carroll Shelf, 1958.
>
> *Little House on the Prairie.* 1935. 335 pp.
>
> *Little Town on the Prairie.* 1941. 307 pp. Awards: Newbery Honor, 1942.
>
> *The Long Winter.* 1940. 335 pp. Awards: Newbery Honor, 1941.
>
> *On the Banks of Plum Creek.* 1937. 339 pp. Awards: Newbery Honor, 1938.
>
> *These Happy Golden Years.* 1943. 289 pp. Awards: Newbery Honor, 1944; Spring Book Festival, 1943.

Historical autobiographical fiction. Gr. 2/3.

Summary: These are stories of the Ingalls family on the American frontier. They begin when Laura is five and continue through her years as a schoolteacher and her marriage to Amos Wilder. The family first lives in Wisconsin, then travels by covered wagon through Kansas, Minnesota, and finally the Dakota territory. The stories tell of hard work, danger, pioneer neighbors, disappoint-ments, sorrow, and celebrations as the three Ingalls girls grow up.

Themes and values: This is a widely known and loved series, portraying a significant part of mainstream American history and values. They are vivid, engrossing stories. For these two reasons they should be familiar to those who work with elementary children. The Ingalls are examples of courage, tenacity, hard work, self-discipline, pride, and strong, loving family life. They are, on occasion, examples of the prejudice and misunderstanding displayed toward native Americans as pioneers moved west. The books are useful resources in the teaching of church history during the 1800s; the importance of Sunday on the frontier; Christmas holidays celebrated with simplicity and joy. Blind Mary's testament of faith in *Little Town on the Prairie*, Ch. 3, is worth sharing with a class or a congregation. A sensitivity to nature is evident throughout the books (for example, *Little House in the Big Woods*, Ch. 13). The children's obedience based on trust in their father illustrates for children a relationship with God; see *Little House on the Prairie*, Ch. 2. In each book there is a chapter on Christmas. These are good resources for ideas on how to hold a simpler, less commercial celebration.

184. Williams, Jay.
Everyone Knows What a Dragon Looks Like.
Illus. by Mercer Mayer. New York: Four Winds, 1976. Awards: Irma Simonton Black, 1977; *New York Times* Best Illustrated, 1976. Picture book, fable. K. unp.

Summary: When fierce warriors threaten, the villagers pray to the Great Cloud Dragon to come and save them. Then a fat, bald little man appears, and everyone—except for one young boy—knows that he could not possibly be the Great Cloud Dragon and look like that. Or could he?

Themes and values: How can you recognize God? How much do our expectations blind us to God at work in the world? A good story, a visual delight, a question about faith and knowledge.

185. Winthrop, Elizabeth. *A Child Is Born.*
Illus. by Charles Mikolaycak. New York: Holiday, 1983. Picture book, text based on the King James Version of the Bible.

Themes and values: Strong, realistic pictures with an oriental touch. A fine book for all ages, an illustration of one kind of art style to interpret the familiar Christmas story.

186. Wojciechowska, Maia. *Shadow of a Bull.*
Illus. by Alvin Smith. New York: Atheneum, 1965. Awards: Newbery, 1965; Spring Book Festival, 1964. Realistic fiction. Gr. 5/6. 165 pp.

Summary: Manolo's father is remembered in the village as a famous bullfighter, so family and friends assume that Manolo will follow in his steps. Manolo must face his fears—of the bull, of failure, of following his own dreams. Through prayer and the wise counsel of those who knew his father best, Manolo finds the courage to decide what is right for him.

Theme and values: A story of confirmation, vocation, achieving maturity. The different cultural setting highlights the universal character of decisions and pressures young people face as they move into adulthood. Manolo's prayer to find the right course of action (ch. 13) can be a valuable section to read in a young people's study on prayer. Contrast Louise's feelings about her parents in *Nobody's Family Is Going to Change* with Manolo's feelings for his. Finding reasons for the difference can be an enlightening exercise.

187. Yagawa, Sumiko. *The Crane Wife.*
Trans. from Japanese by Katherine Paterson. Illus. by Suekichi Akaba. New York: William Morrow, 1981. Awards: *New York Times* Best Illustrated, 1981. Japanese folk tale; picture book with pictures adding immeasurably to the poignant story. K. unp.

Summary: A simple peasant tends a wounded crane; late that night, a beautiful young woman appears at the door and asks to be his wife. She weaves exquisite cloth as they need money, but forbids her husband to watch her weave. His greed and curiosity destroy their happy relationship.

Themes and values: This is a universal theme expressed through an ageless folk tale. We all need to understand what greed and selfishness can do to selfless love. Here that experience is reduced to its verbal and visual essence. No comments or discussions need to follow.

188. Yashima, Taro. *Crow Boy.*
Illus. by author. New York: Viking, 1955. Awards: Caldecott Honor, 1956; Child Study, 1955. Picture/story book. Gr. 1. 37 pp.

Summary: Chibi seems a person of no importance, even an object of ridicule. But Mr. Isobe, his sixth-grade teacher, takes time to find out something about him. Everyone is surprised when Chibi appears on the stage at the talent show with a special ability.

Themes and values: A picture of social isolation based on superficial judgment; the worth of unique abilities and talents; the importance of a supporting, observing adult; perseverance. An outstanding example of pictures and text reinforcing one another. Moving and beautifully written.

189. Yates, Elizabeth. *Amos Fortune: Free Man.*
Illus. by Nora S. Unwin. New York: E.P. Dutton, 1950. Awards: Newbery, 1951; Spring Book Festival, 1950; William Allen White, 1953. Biographical, historical fiction, colonial America. Gr. 4/5. 181 pp.

Summary: Amos Fortune was born an African prince, was captured and sold as a slave, and became a tanner in colonial America. His original owners were Quakers who treated him as a member of the family and taught him to read and write, using the Bible. His passion was for freedom, and he worked first to buy his own freedom, then the freedom of other slaves.

Themes and values: Currently this book is being criticized for what is interpreted as a passive attitude on Amos Fortune's part toward the evil of slavery. Through patience, fortitude, sacrifice, work, prayer, and faith, Fortune in his own way accomplished a small revolution.

190. Yep, Laurence. *Dragonwings.*
New York: Harper and Row, 1975. Awards: ALA Notable, 1975; Newbery Honor, 1976; *Globe-Horn*, 1976; Lewis Carroll Shelf, 1979; International Reading Assn., 1976; Carter G. Woodson, 1976. Fiction, 1903-1919, California. Gr. 5/6. 248 pp.

Summary: In 1903 a young boy travels from China to join a father he has never met. Windrider, the father, is a man of imagination and dreams. Although the life of the Chinese in the Land of the Golden Mountain is hard, still the new land offers Windrider opportunity, and he builds a flying machine with the help of his son and newfound friends.

Themes and values: A good historical portrayal of San Francisco, the 1906 earthquake, the life and work of the Chinese who arrived in America. A testimony to hope's transforming a difficult life; the unhappiness of those who have nothing to believe in; the beauty and nobility of moments when we share in working toward a goal with others. Yep's work helps us see and appreciate cultural differences and universal joys and dreams. His *Child of the Owl* is a contemporary story of a young American girl's need to find identity through the appreciation of her Chinese heritage.

191. ———. *The Serpent's Children.*
New York: Harper and Row, 1984. Realistic, historical fiction. Gr. 6. 277 pp.

Summary: Cassia fights to keep her home and family as her mother dies and her father returns from war a crippled and beaten man. Their home has been the center of the Work, a revolutionary movement which will free China from Manchu and British domination. But the Work now involves robbery and oppression rather than brotherhood. Foxfire, Cassia's brother, seeks his dream in America, while Cassia's father comes to terms with a tarnished vision.

Themes and values: Increased understanding of Chinese Americans, a picture of a movement based on high ideals that fail. Katherine Paterson's *Rebels of the Heavenly Kingdom* treats this same movement in its early stages from the perspective of two young members. In combination the two books make a thought-provoking statement about the dangers inherent in even the loftiest of goals pursued by an organized movement, about how easily means destroy ends.

192. **Yolen, Jane.** *Children of the Wolf.*
New York: Viking Press, 1984. Based on an actual and controversial account of feral children in India in the 1920s. Gr. 5. 136 pp.

Summary: Two human children found in the den of a she-wolf are taken to a Christian orphanage in India. The effort to bring them from their wild state into the human community becomes the personal story of Mohandas, a fourteen-year-old inmate at the orphanage. He sees in their alienation a reflection of his own loneliness. He tries to protect the wolf girls from the cruelty of the other children at the orphanage, but comes to realize, finally, that he has a priceless treasure which it is too late to impart to Amala and Kamala—the gift of words.

Themes and values: Poignant illustration of the importance of language and early environment. A look at Indian culture and some of the effects of Christian missions. The idea of vocation and the use of talent are explored, briefly, at the end of the book.

193. **Zolotow, Charlotte.** *The Hating Book.*
Illus. by Ben Shecter. New York: Harper and Row, 1969. Picture book. P. 32 pp.

Summary: When your best friend begins to ignore you, naturally you feel angry. The hateful feelings that begin to be generated can be resolved only by an open encounter to learn the reasons for rejection.

Themes and values: When a relationship breaks down, the best thing to do is talk with your friend. Psychologically sound, this slight story accepts anger; reflects the emotionally debilitating character of hatred; includes an objective, helpful adult; and gives some obvious steps in peacemaking. *Harriet the Spy* explores some of these same ramifications on another level.

194. ———. *The Quarreling Book.*
Illus. by Arnold Lobel. New York: Harper and Row, 1963. Picture book. P. unp.

Summary: The day is gray and rainy; Mr. James forgets to kiss Mrs. James good-bye; Mrs. James is cross with Jonathan, who in turn mistreats his sister, etc. The sequence is reversed when Eddie's little dog licks him regardless of the treatment he has received.

Themes and values: The consequence of actions; changing the course of actions; peacemaking. This is one way young children grasp concepts. Single actions and results are connected in a very direct way. Zolotow is an author gifted in making concepts simple and portraying children's dreams and emotions, i.e. *When I Have a Little Girl, If It Weren't for You, Over and Over.* Any of these books would be a valuable addition for the preschool classroom.

Other Books Mentioned in the Text

Aiken, Joan. *Black Hearts in Battersea.*
Illus. by Robin Jacques. Garden City, NY: Doubleday, 1964.

Blume, Judy. *Superfudge.*
Illus. by Roy Doty. New York: E.P. Dutton, 1980. Popular author, limited style.

———. *Tales of a Fourth Grade Nothing.*
Illus. by Roy Doty. New York: E.P. Dutton, 1972.

Burnford, Sheila. *The Incredible Journey.*
Illus. by Carl Burger. Boston: Little, Brown, 1960.

Hutchins, Pat. *Rosie's Walk*.
New York: Macmillan, 1968. The story on filmstrip is from Weston Woods, 1971.

L'Engle, Madeleine. *A Wrinkle in Time*.
New York: Farrar, Straus, Giroux, 1962.

Nesbit, Edith. *Edith Nesbit: Five Children and It* [1902]; *The Phoenix and the Carpet* [1904]; *The Story of the Amulet* [1906].
Illus. by H. R. Miller. London: Octopus, 1979.

Rawls, Wilson. *Where the Red Fern Grows*.
Garden City, NY: Doubleday, 1961. Popular, inferior style.

Warner, Gertrude. *The Boxcar Children*.
Chicago: Whitman, 1945. Popular, limited characters, plot, and style.

12

Children's Book Awards

ALA Notable Books. A short list of about 50 titles chosen for their outstanding qualities. Annual.

Jane Addams Book Award. For the book which best promotes peace, dignity, and equality for all people, as well as social justice. Annual.

American Book Award. To recognize and award books of artistic and literary merit. Annual.

American Institute of Graphic Arts Book Show. The show presents a variety of American publishing, in order to recognize and encourage distinguished graphic work in many different forms. Annual.

Hans Christian Andersen Award. To an international author and to an illustrator who have made a lasting contribution to literature for youth. Their complete works are taken into consideration. Annual.

Art Books for Children Citations. To highlight outstanding verbal and visual achievement in children's books. Annual.

Aurianne Award. Best book about animals. Criterion is the book's ability to instill a humane attitude toward animals.

Australian Children's Book Award. Given for the best illustrated children's book. Annual.

Irma Simonton Black Award. Given to a book for young children that was published during the preceding year; award is based on excellence of text and graphics. Annual.

Boston Globe—Horn *Book Award.* Given for outstanding fiction, outstanding nonfiction, and outstanding illustration. Annual.

Boys' Club Junior Book Award. This award was given to books that encouraged wider reading among members of Boys' Clubs. Now discontinued.

Randolph Caldecott Medal. To the artist of the most distinguished American picture book for children published in the U.S. in the preceding year. Annual.

Carnegie Medal. Outstanding book for children, written in English and published in the United Kingdom during preceding year. Annual.

Lewis Carroll Shelf Award. For those titles that possess enough of the qualities of *Alice in Wonderland* to enable them to stand on the same book shelf. Annual.

Child Study Children's Book Award. To a book that deals realistically and in a positive way with problems in the world of children. Annual.

Children's Book Showcase. For outstanding qualities of design and production. Annually from 1972–1977.

Christopher Award. Books that provide affirmation of the highest values of the human spirit. Annual.

Commonwealth Club of California Writers Award. Given only to California residents for best juvenile titles of the year. Annual.

Garden State Children's Book Award. For early and middle grade books that encourage, stimulate, and captivate potential readers. New Jersey. Annual.

Georgia Children's Book Award. Children's Choice. Annual.

Esther Glen Award. This award is given to the New Zealand children's book author whose literature is considered to be the most distinguished of the year. Annual.

Golden Archer Award. Wisconsin children's choice. Annual.

Golden Kite Award. For titles which exhibit excellence in writing and genuinely appeal to the interests and concerns of children. Annual

Kate Greenaway Medal. Awarded to an artist who has produced the most distinguished work in the illustration of a children's book published in the preceding year in the United Kingdom. Annual.

Sue Hefly Award. Louisiana children's choice. Annual.

International Board on Books for Young People (IBBY) Honor List. Includes no more than three books from each member country, chosen for excellence in writing, illustration, and translation. Books are recommended as suitable for publication throughout the world to encourage world understanding through children's literature. Every two years.

International Reading Association Children's Book Award. Awarded to an author's first or second title for a juvenile audience. Annual.

Iowa Children's Choice Award. The purpose of the award is to encourage children to read more and better books; to discriminate in choosing worthwhile books; to provide an avenue for positive dialogue between teacher, parent, and children about books and authors. Nominations are accepted from students, teachers, media specialists, and administrators. Annual.

Clara Ingram Judson Award. Sponsored by the society of Midland authors. Now discontinued.

Massachusetts Children's Book Award. Children's choice. Annual.

National Book Award. Now replaced by the American Book Awards. For the most distinguished book written by an American citizen and published in the U.S. for children.

Nene Award. Hawaii children's choice. Annual.

New Jersey Institute of Technology New Jersey Authors Award. To honor New Jersey authors and noteworthy books. Annual.

New York Times *Choice of Best Illustrated Children's Books of the Year.* To honor the highest quality illustrations in children's books. Annual.

John Newbery Medal. Presented to the author of the most distinguished contribution to American literature for children published in the U.S. for the preceding year. Annual.

North Carolina Division of American Association of University Women's Award in Juvenile Literature. For outstanding work of a North Carolina author.

Other Award. An alternative children's book award given to non-biased books of literary merit published in Great Britain from July 1 to July 30, including reprints and paperback editions.

Sequoyah Children's Book Award. Oklahoma children's choice. Annual.

South Carolina Children's Book Award. Children's choice. Annual.

Southern California Council on Literature for Children and Young People Award. The awards recognize outstanding books, illustrations, and bodies of work by Southern Californians. Annual.

Spring Book Festival Award. To encourage excellence in children's book publishing, 1937–1973. Discontinued.

George G. Stone Center Recognition of Merit Award. For a book or body of works that has the capacity to arouse an awareness of the complexity and beauty of the universe. Annual.

Surrey School Book of the Year Award. Children's choice. Annual.

Texas Bluebonnet Award. Children's choice.

Tir-na-n′ Og. Given to an outstanding book published in the English language with an authentic Welsh background.

Mark Twain Award. Missouri children's choice. Annual.

William Allen White Children's Book Award. Kansas children's choice. Annual.

Laura Ingalls Wilder Award. Presented to an author or illustrator whose books have made a lasting and substantial contribution to children's literature over a period of time.

Carter G. Woodson Book Award. The award is to encourage the writing, publishing, and dissemination of outstanding social science books for young readers that treat topics related to ethnic minorities and race relations sensitively and accurately. Annual.

Young Hoosier Award. Indiana children's choice. For the book that best stimulates the recreational reading of upper elementary children. Annual.

Young Reader's Choice Award. Children's choice conducted in Alaska, Alberta, British Columbia, Idaho, Montana, Oregon, and Washington. Annual.

Young Reader Medal. A readers' choice award given by the California Reading Association from a list of titles nominated by students and voted on by grades K–12. Titles must have been written in the last five years by an author who is still alive.

13

Resources for Leaders

Of the making of many books about children's literature there is no end. This selection contains books we have liked and used. Some we own; some we use at a public library. Not everyone has easy access to a library, so we will indicate a bare-bones book list to purchase. At the end is a list in which we have grouped the books according to use and have indicated with an asterisk (*) which one in that section is the starting point if there is a clear choice.

Bibliography for Adults

Aiken, Joan. *The Way to Write for Children*. New York: St. Martin's, 1982. Pb. A 93-page guide by a prize-winning author, but the book is not just for potential authors. The craft of writing, the elements of a good book, the interests and the reading style of children are presented in nine brisk, easy-to-ready chapters.

Bauer, Caroline Feller. *This Way to Books*. Drawings by Lynn Gates. New York: H. W. Wilson, 1983. A collection of programs and ideas that will stimulate a child's interest in books. It is a potpourri, designed to allow the reader to pick and choose items for particular situations. It presents an interesting mini-course outline on how to teach volunteers to tell stories; program formats that can be adapted for a number of occasions; good techniques for giving booktalks; and selected titles to use in each case. Chapters on games, crafts, and exhibits as well as the program themes may spark ideas for church school learning centers, for intergenerational activities related to books, or for fairs and festivals. Buy it—it is worth every penny.

Bennett, Gordon C. *Readers Theatre Comes to the Church*. Atlanta: John Knox Press, 1972. Pb. A guide both to adapting stories, book sections, and Bible stories for readers theater, and to the techniques for effective reading and staging. Practical, clear, a tested and proven aid. Out of print, but try to find it.

Bettelheim, Bruno. *The Uses of Enchantment: The Meaning and Importance of Fairy Tales*. New York: Alfred A. Knopf, 1976. The importance of fairy tales in the nurture of character and imagination is the emphasis that is helpful in this book by an expert in child psychology.

Blishen, Edward, ed. *The Thorny Paradise: Writers on Writing for Children*. Middlesex, England: Penguin, 1975. Jill Paton Walsh, Helen Cresswell, Ursula Le Guin, John Gordon, and Richard Adams are a few of the authors who share their reasons for writing and their feelings about children in this rich volume.

Bodart, Joni. *Booktalk! Booktalking and School Visiting for Young Adult Audiences*. New York: H. W. Wilson, 1980. Well over half the book is composed of actual booktalks, but the first eighty-five pages are devoted to methods and techniques for giving successful booktalks. It is useful to anyone desiring to use this way of sharing books.

Cameron, Eleanor. *The Green and Burning Tree: On the Writing and Enjoyment of Children's Books*. Boston: Little, Brown, 1962. Critical essays by a gifted author. The first section on fantasy, and the chapters on style and audience are especially stimulating. Not the first book to read.

Child Study Children's Book Committee at Bank Street College. *Paperback Books for Children: A Selected List Through Age Twelve*. New York: Child Study Children's Book Committee, Bank Street College of Education, 1983. An inexpensive, useful, thirty-page resource listing over five hundred titles. It usually eliminates the need for consulting the complete guide to paperback books on the library reference shelves.

Cianciolo, Patricia Jean. *Picture Books for Children.* Chicago: American Library Association, 1981. 2d ed. Pb. The introduction gives the novice an overview of styles, masters of each style, things to look for in picture books, and what children appreciate and enjoy. The bulk of the book is an annotated list of outstanding picture books grouped by four themes: Me and My Family, Other People, The World I Live In, and The Imaginative World. Sample illustrations are in black and white only.

Dreyer, Sharon Spredemann, ed. *The Bookfinder: A Guide to Children's Literature about the Needs and Problems of Youth Aged 2–15.* 2 vols. Circle Pines, MN: American Guidance Service, 1977, 1981. A split-page format. The top half lists 450 topics such as values, self-esteem, family conflict, etc., in children's fiction; the bottom half lists the books with summary and age level. Vol. 1 annotates 1,131 books; Vol. 2, 723. Very useful and very expensive. It can be found on many library reference shelves.

Duran, Daniel Flores. *Latino Materials: A Multimedia Guide for Children and Young Adults.* Santa Barbara, CA: American Biographical Center, 1979. Listings include both English and Spanish resources.

Ettlinger, John R. T., and Diana Spirt. *Choosing Books for Young People: A Guide to Criticism and Bibliography, 1945–1975.* Chicago: American Library Association, 1982. A listing of the guides to children's literature that have existed between 1945 and 1975. It includes those guides still useful for current book selection and reevaluation and comments on the purpose for which each guide is best suited. Subject index may provide access to specific topics such as non-sexist materials, socially handicapped children, and intercultural understanding.

Frye, Northrop. *The Great Code: The Bible and Literature.* New York: Harcourt Brace Jovanovich, 1982. Among other things, Frye shows the impact of the Bible on literary forms and the creative imagination in western civilization. The idea is also touched on in a much briefer book, *The Educated Imagination.* Bloomington, IN: Indiana University, 1964. Not for casual reading, but important.

Gillespie, John T., and Christine B. Gilbert, eds. *Best Books for Children.* 2d ed. New York: R. R. Bowker, 1981. A comprehensive list of 13,000 titles, arranged by subject: arts, holidays, ethnic, maturity, family life, etc., with a short description of each book.

Haviland, Virginia, ed. *Children and Literature: Views and Reviews.* New York: Lothrop, Lee, Shepard, 1973. Articles covering every aspect of this subject from history to present trends. The most noted authors, illustrators, and critics are included in this collection. Natalie Babbitt, Robert Burch, and Nicholas Tucker have valuable chapters. Lewis' "On Three Ways of Writing for Children" is included in this volume.

Hearne, Betsy. *Choosing Books for Children: A Commonsense Guide.* New York: Delacorte, 1981. Pb. A very personal listing of favorite books in different age categories by a professional children's book reviewer. Her selections are guided by a thorough knowledge of the children's book field and daily experience in judging and evaluating new material. A brief book, containing 100 sure-fire selections.

Hunt, Mary Alice, ed. *A Multimedia Approach to Children's Literature: A selective list of films and videocassettes, filmstrips, and recordings based on children's books.* 3d ed. Pb. Chicago: American Library Association, 1983. 182 pp. Directory of distributors, Spanish language versions, bibliography of nonprint materials about authors. A useful reference book for a church.

Jones, Dolores Blythe. *Children's Literature Awards and Winners: A Directory of Prizes, Authors, and Illustrators.* 1st ed. Detroit: Neal-Schuman in association with Gale Research Co., 1983. A listing of the major awards in children's literature in English, divided into three parts: directory of awards and winning titles; award-winning authors and illustrators, titles of winning books, with all awards for each title listed; selected bibliography of topics germane to children's book awards. The cost is $75, so look for this book on your local library reference shelf.

Karl, Jean. *From Childhood to Childhood: Children's Books and Their Creators.* New York: John Day, 1970. An editor at Atheneum, Karl speaks with special fervor about the value of children's literature to children. Includes information about editing and publishing juvenile books, and a good chapter on how adults should read these books.

Kimmel, Margaret Mary, and Elizabeth Segel. *For Reading Out Loud! A Guide To Sharing Books with Children.* New York: Delacorte, 1983. An introductory section tells why and how, followed by a list of 140 books, summarized with suggestions for time required and snags to avoid. The books are cross-listed under such titles as One-Session Reads, Surefire, Wide Age-Range, Stay-at-Homes, and Travellers (by geographic location).

Larrick, Nancy. *A Parent's Guide to Children's Reading.* 5th ed. Philadelphia: Westminster, 1982. A completely revised edition of an old classic that has been a treasured resource for parents and grandparents since 1958. Larrick gives the rationale for using books in the home and lists favorite titles for all ages and across many subjects. For parents and others who want to give more than casual guidance to children's reading.

L'Engle, Madeleine. *Walking On Water: Reflections on Faith and Art*. New York: Bantam, 1980. Pb. An articulate Christian author and Newbery winner writes informally about the relationship of faith and art. A book to stimulate thinking.

Lewis, C.S. *An Experiment in Criticism*. Cambridge, England: Cambridge University, 1961. The way the book is read and the readers who return to it are the bases for judging books. An eloquent statement of the value of literature and reading.

———. *Of Other Worlds: Essays and Stories*. Ed. by Walter Hooper. New York: Harcourt, Brace, World, 1966. Several essays in this volume are concerned with children's literature and Lewis' own approach to writing. Of special interest are those about fairy stories, the writing of the Narnia series, juvenile taste, and "On Three Ways of Writing for Children."

Lewis, Claudia. *Writing for Young Children*. Rev. ed. Garden City, NY: Doubleday, 1981. Most of the ideas in this book are helpful for oral or written communication with any age. Lewis emphasizes impression first, then expression through the language of sensory impression.

Lima, Carolyn W. *A to Zoo: Subject Access to Children's Picture Books*. New York: R. R. Bowker, 1982. Preschool picture books (4,400) are classified by subject.

Lukens, Rebecca J. *A Critical Handbook of Children's Literature*. 2d ed. Glenville, IL: Scott Foresman, 1982. Writing out of the conviction that children's literature should be judged by the same standards as writing for adults, Lukens explores genre, character, plot, setting, point of view, style, tone, and theme, as well as criticism of poetry and nonfiction. Her points are illustrated with numerous examples from children's literature.

Ott, Helen Keating. *Helping Children Through Books*. Bryn Mawr, PA: Church and Synagogue Library Association, 1979. A selected list, age graded, on such topics as living with self, living with others, broadening friendships, hospital, death, religion, drugs, ecology, and homosexuality.

Paterson, Katherine. *Gates of Excellence: On Reading and Writing Books for Children*. New York: Elsevier/Nelson, 1981. Two Newbery Awards and two National Book Awards suggest that Paterson is an author who knows her craft. This is also a book about values, standards, and the relationship of author and reader.

Paulin, Mary Ann. *Creative Uses of Children's Literature*. Hamden, CT: Library Professional Publications, 1982. 730 pp. This comprehensive book is very useful because of its extensive subject bibliography, listing such topics as abandonment, wisdom, worry, self-satisfaction, and physical handicaps along with the page numbers where the appropriate titles appear. It is full of ideas which could be adapted for Christian education, but there is so much material that it is easy to be overwhelmed. It demands time and careful perusal. Pages 345–50 contain listings and comments about prayers and hymns, children's Bibles and Bible stories, and the nativity in story and verse. Ch. 5, "Playing Stories," gives good, practical information about using creative dramatics and puppets.

Pearl, Patricia. *Religious Books for Children: An Annotated Bibliography*. Bryn Mawr, PA: Church and Synagogue Library Association, 1983. 36 pp. Pb. Books for preschool and elementary children, organized by the following subjects: Bible, Old Testament, New Testament, Christian Theology, Church, Judaism, Religion, and Religious Holidays. A necessary resource for church libraries and education. Excludes fiction except where related to the Bible or to a character in church history.

Polette, Nancy, and Marjorie Hamlin. *Celebrating with Books*. Metuchen, NJ: Scarecrow, 1977. 175 pp. Ten holidays, and books and activities to go with them. Many would enrich Christian education programs.

Rudman, Masha Kabakow. *Children's Literature: An Issues Approach*. Lexington, MA: D.C. Heath, 1976. The issues are: Siblings, Divorce, Death and Old Age, War, Sex, The Black, The Native American, and The Female. Each chapter discusses the treatment of the issue in current children's literature. An annotated list of books on these topics is included. Further activities for children are suggested.

Scherf, Walter, ed. *The Best of the Best: Picture, Children's, and Youth Books from 110 Countries or Languages*. New York: R. R. Bowker, 1976. A selection of the best youth and children's books in many languages. The basic idea of the work is to promote understanding of different ways of life. The books selected for the U.S. entry could be matched against other lists of "best" books when devising a canon or basic list of recognized children's books.

Sutherland, Zena, Dianne L. Monson, and May Hill Arbuthnot. *Children and Books*. 6th ed. Glenview, IL: Scott, Foresman, 1981. A textbook for colleges, a standard resource since 1947. An introduction to child development and children's literature, an overview of picture books, an anthology of stories and poems, detailed evaluations of contemporary fiction and nonfiction, ways of encouraging and developing reading, and issues in children's reading and juvenile book publishing today. A valuable reference book.

Trelease, Jim. *The Read-aloud Handbook*. New York: Penguin, 1982. Pb. The case for reading aloud is presented with missionary zeal, partly because it enhances the child's desire and ability to master reading skills. Three hundred books are annotated.

White, Mary Lou. *Children's Literature: Criticism and Response*. Columbus, OH: Charles E. Merrill, 1976. A collection of essays illustrating four ways in which a work may be critically evaluated: psychologically, sociologically, structurally, and according to archetypal elements. The thesis is that children can be helped to respond to literature in each of these four ways. Suggestions for leading children into an understanding of these components are included at the end of each section.

A Guide to Using the Adult Bibliography

Background Readings

Bettelheim, *The Uses of Enchantment*
Frye, *The Educated Imagination, The Great Code*
L'Engle, *Walking on Water*
Lewis, *An Experiment in Criticism*

Getting an Overview

Cianciolo, *Picture Books for Children*
Haviland, *Children and Literature*
Hearne, *Choosing Books for Children*
Karl, *From Childhood to Childhood**
Larrick, *A Parent's Guide to Children's Reading*
Sutherland et al., *Children and Books,* Part I

The Writer's Viewpoint

Aiken, *The Way to Write for Children**
Blishen, *The Thorny Paradise*
Lewis, C. S., *Of Other Worlds*
Lewis, Claudia, *Writing for Young Children*
Paterson, *Gates of Excellence*

Developing Judgment

Cameron, *The Green and Burning Tree*

Lukens, *A Critical Handbook of Children's Literature**
Jones, *Children's Literature Awards and Winners*
White, *Children's Literature: Criticism and Response*

Finding Books: General Bibliographies

Gillespie and Gilbert, *Best Books for Children**
Larrick, *A Parent's Guide to Children's Reading*
Scherf, *The Best of the Best*

Finding Books by Subject

Ettlinger and Spirt, *Choosing Books for Young People*
Lima, *A to Zoo*

Special Subjects

Latino Materials
Duran, *Latino Materials*

Needs and Problems
Dreyer, *The Bookfinder**
Ott, *Helping Children Through Books*
Rudman, *Children's Literature: An Issues Approach*

Religion and Bible
Pearl, *Religious Books for Children*

Types of Books

Paperback Books
Child Study, Bank Street, *Paperback Books for Children*

Picture Books
Cianciolo, *Picture Books for Children*

Read-aloud Books
Kimmel and Segel, *For Reading Out Loud!**
Trelease, *The Read-aloud Handbook*

Using Books

Bauer, *This Way to Books**
Bennett, *Readers Theatre Comes to the Church*
Bodart, *Booktalk!*
Hunt, *A Multimedia Approach*
Paulin, *Creative Uses of Children's Literature*
Polette and Hamlin, *Celebrating with Books*

The Basic Library

Sutherland, et al., *Children and Books*
Bauer, *This Way to Books*

Addresses and Ordering Information for Periodicals, Monographs, etc.

Association for Library Services to Children, a division of American Library Association, 50 East Huron St., Chicago, IL 60611. ALA publishes an annual list of materials for sale. The source for the annual Notable Books list. A good resource for parents and the church library. Order *Booklist,* an every other week periodical, from this address.

Building a Children's Literature Collection, 3d ed., by Harriet B. Quimby and Margaret Mary Kimmel. Order from *Choice* Bibliographical Essay Series, #7, 1983. 100 Riverview Center, Middletown, CT 06457.

Children's Books Awards and Prizes, compiled and edited by Children's Book Council, 1981. $10.95. Order from Children's Book Council, Inc., 67 Irving Place, New York, NY 10003.

Children's Literature Center, Library of Congress, Washington, DC 20540. The Center compiles and publishes a list of materials, available through the Superintendent of Documents. Among them, *The Best of Children's Books*, 1980; *Children's Books,* a selected annual list of new books; and *Children and Poetry*, 1979, a selective annotated bibliography.

Church and Synagogue Libraries. Church and Synagogue Library Association, P.O. Box 1130, Bryn Mawr, PA 19010. A bi-monthly bulletin with articles and book comments. A sample copy will be sent on request. This address is the source for *Religious Books for Children,* a very useful annotated bibliography; *Helping Children Through Books*; guides on library standards, classifying and cataloguing books, and other subjects.

The Horn Book Magazine. Horn Book, Inc., Park Square Bldg., 31 St. James Ave., Boston, MA 02116. Current reviews; recommended books; articles about children and young adults. Six issues yearly, $27.

New York Public Library, The Office of Branch Libraries, 455 5th Ave., New York, NY 10016, will send you a list of its publications for purchase. Of note are *Children's Books* (100 titles), annual; *Books for the Teen Age,* annual; *The Black Experience in Children's Books*, 1984.

New York Times Book Review. Subscription sales: P.O. Box 508, Hackensack, NJ 07602–9983. Weekly, $22/yr.

Publisher's Weekly. R. R. Bowker Co., Subscription Dept., Box 1428, Riverton, NJ 08077. Weekly, $78/yr. Order *School Library Journal,* a monthly publication (except June and July) from Subscription Dept., Box 1426, Riverton, NJ 08077. For children's, young adult, and school librarians. $47/yr.

Reference List

Aiken, Joan. 1982. *The Way to Write for Children.* New York: St. Martin's.

————. 1976. "Writing for Enjoyment." Pages 15–26 in *Writers, Critics, and Children: Articles from Children's Literature in Education.* Edited by Geoff Fox et al. New York: Agathon.

Ausubel, David. 1980. *Theory and Problems of Child Development.* 3rd ed. Orlando, FL: Crune and Stratton.

Babbitt, Natalie. 1973. "Happy Endings? Of Course, and Also Joy." Pages 155–59 in *Children and Literature: Views and Reviews.* Edited by Virginia Haviland. New York: Lothrop, Lee, Shepard.

Bowley, Agatha. 1966. *The Natural Development of the Child: A Guide for Parents, Teachers, Students, and Others.* London: E & S Livingstone.

Buechner, Frederick. 1977. *Telling the Truth: The Gospel as Tragedy, Comedy, and Fairy Tale.* New York: Harper and Row.

Buttrick, David G. 1983. "On Preaching a Parable: The Problem of a Homiletic Method." *Reformed Liturgy and Music* 17:16–22.

Calvino, Italo. 1980. *Italian Folktales* (Selected and Retold). Trans. by George Martin. New York: Harcourt Brace Jovanovich.

Cameron, Eleanor. 1962. *The Green and Burning Tree: On the Writing and Enjoyment of Children's Books.* Boston: Little, Brown.

Chambers, Aidan. 1973. *Introducing Books to Children.* London: Heinemann.

Craddock, Fred B. 1979. *As One Without Authority.* 3rd ed. Nashville: Abingdon.

Erikson, Erik H. 1964. *Childhood and Society.* 2nd ed. New York: Norton.

Furnish, Dorothy Jean. 1975. *Exploring the Bible with Children.* Nashville: Abingdon.

Groome, Thomas H. 1980. *Christian Religious Education: Sharing Our Story and Vision.* San Francisco: Harper & Row.

Gruber, Howard E., and J. Jacques Vonèche, eds. 1977. *The Essential Piaget*. New York: Basic Books.

Hearne, Betsy. 1981. *Choosing Books for Children: A Commonsense Guide*. New York: Delacorte.

Huck, Charlotte S. 1979. *Children's Literature in the Elementary School*. 3rd rev. ed. New York: Holt, Rinehart, Winston.

Johnson, James Weldon. *God's Trombones*. Recording by Bryce Bond, Folkways/Scholastic Records.

Kipling, Rudyard. 1912. *Just So Stories*. Illus. by J.M. Gleeson. New York: Doubleday.

Krumgold, Joseph. 1967. "Why Write Books for Children?" The Chicago *Tribune Children's Book World*, November 5, 1967, 2.

L'Engle, Madeleine. 1980. *Walking on Water: Reflections on Faith and Art*. Wheaton, IL: Harold Shaw.

Lewis, C.S. 1961. *An Experiment in Criticism*. Cambridge, England: Cambridge University.

———. 1966. *Of Other Worlds: Essays and Stories*. New York: Harcourt, Brace, World.

Lewis, Claudia. 1981. *Writing for Young Children*. Rev. ed. Garden City, NY: Anchor/Doubleday.

Long, Thomas G. 1983. "The Distance We Have Traveled: Changing Trends in Preaching." *Reformed Liturgy and Music* 17: 11–15.

Maslow, Abraham H., ed. 1970. *Motivation and Personality*. 2nd ed. New York: Harper and Row.

Nichols, J. Randall. 1980. *Building the Word: The Dynamics of Communication and Preaching*. San Francisco: Harper and Row.

Paterson, Katherine. 1981. *Gates of Excellence: On Reading and Writing Books for Children*. New York: Elsevier/Nelson.

Walsh, Jill Paton. 1975. "Seeing Green." In *The Thorny Paradise: Writers on Writing for Children*. Edited by Edward Blishen. Middlesex, England: Penguin.

Woodward, Kenneth L., with Margaret Moorman. 1984. "Inspirational Romances," *Newsweek*, Feb. 20, 1984, 69.

Note: all other references are in the Bibliography "Books for All Ages."

Index of Themes and Subjects in Bibliography*

*The numbers following entries refer to bibliography entry numbers rather than page numbers.

Index of Genre

Index to Children's Book Awards